Ten Great Sermons
from
Basil to Calvin

Ten Great Sermons
from
Basil to Calvin

COMPILED BY

GRENVILLE KLEISER

Formerly of Yale Divinity School Faculty;
Author of " How to Speak
in Public," Etc.

With Assistance from Many of the Foremost
Living Preachers and Other Theologians

INTRODUCTION BY

LEWIS O. BRASTOW, D.D.

Professor Emeritus of Practical Theology
in Yale University

WIPF & STOCK · Eugene, Oregon

Wipf and Stock Publishers
199 W 8th Ave, Suite 3
Eugene, OR 97401

Ten Great Sermons from Basil to Calvin
By Kleiser, Grenville and Brastow, Lewis O.
ISBN 13: 978-1-5326-1300-5
Publication date 10/21/2016
Previously published as The World's Great Sermons,
Volume 1 – Basil to Calvin
by Funk & Wagnalls Company, 1908

PREFACE

THE aim in preparing this work has been to bring together the best examples of the products of the pulpit through the Christian centuries, and to present these masterpieces in attractive and convenient form. It is believed that they will be found valuable as instruction to ministers of to-day. They should also be helpful to others who, tho not preachers, yet seek reading of this kind for the upbuilding of personal character and for strengthening their Christian faith.

The sermons have been chosen in some cases for their literary and rhetorical excellences, but in every case for their helpfulness in solving some of the problems of Christian living. No two persons are likely to agree upon "the best" of anything, and readers will probably wish in particular instances that

PREFACE

some other clergymen or sermons had been included. It is confidently believed, however, that the list here given is fairly representative of the preaching that characterized the age to which each sermon respectively belongs.

While some of the sermons of the early centuries may not seem exactly fitted to modern needs, it is thought that those presented will repay careful perusal, since they each contain a distinct message for later generations. Moreover, a comparison extending over the whole field of sermonic literature, such as the preacher may make with this collection before him, should prove most valuable as showing what progress and changes have come over homiletic matter and methods. Such a comparison should in fact throw much light on the spirit and conditions of various homiletic periods.

In choosing sermons by living preachers considerable difficulty has been found, not only in deciding upon sermons, but upon preachers. The list might have been extended

PREFACE

indefinitely. Whenever possible the preacher, when living, has himself been consulted as to what he considered his most representative sermon.

Thanks are due, and are hereby acknowledged, to numerous clergymen, publishers, librarians, and others who have generously assisted the compiler in this undertaking. Most grateful acknowledgment is also made to the Rev. Epiphanius Wilson and the Rev. W. C. Stiles for valuable editorial assistance.

GRENVILLE KLEISER.

New York City, October, 1908.

INTRODUCTION

COLLECTIONS of sermons by noted preachers of different periods are not an altogether uncommon contribution to literature. Italy, Germany, Holland, France, Great Britain and the United States have in this way furnished copious illustrations of the gifts of their illustrious preachers. Such treasures are found in the Latin and even in the Greek Church. Protestant communions especially, in line with the supreme significance which they attach to the work of the pulpit, have thus sought to magnify the calling and to perpetuate the memory and the influence of their distinguished sons. Still more comprehensive attempts have been made to collate the products of representative preachers in different Protestant communions, and thus to bring into prominence various types of sermonic literature. It is in this

INTRODUCTION

way that the Christian world has come to know its pulpit princes and to value their achievements.

The collection contained in the volumes before us is, however, more varied and comprehensive, reaching as it does from the fourth to the twentieth century, than any collection known to the writer. In the selection Professor Kleiser has brought to his task a personal knowledge of homiletic literature that is the product of much observation and study during many years, and an enthusiasm for his work that has been fostered by close intercourse in professional service with preachers and theological students. He has had the assistance also of men whose acquaintance with homiletic literature is very extensive, whose critical judgments are sound and reliable and who may be regarded as experts in this branch of knowledge. These volumes, therefore, may be accepted as a judiciously selected collection of sermons by many of the most notable preachers of the ancient and

INTRODUCTION

modern Christian world. Their value as illustrating varieties of gift, diversities of method, racial, national and ecclesiastical peculiarities, and above all progress in the science and art of preaching, may well be recognized even by a generation that is likely to regard anything that is more than twenty-four hours old as obsolete.

LEWIS O. BRASTOW.

Yale University, New Haven, Conn., October, 1908.

CONTENTS

VOLUME I

	Page
PREFACE	v
INTRODUCTION	ix

BASIL (329—379).
    The Creation of the World . . . 1

CHRYSOSTOM (347—407).
    Excessive Grief at the Death of Friends 23

AUGUSTINE (354—430).
    The Recovery of Sight by the Blind . 47

WYCLIF (1324—1384).
    Christ's Real Body Not in the Eucharist 73

SAVONAROLA (1452—1498).
    The Ascension of Christ 91

LUTHER (1483—1546).
    The Method and Fruits of Justification 113

LATIMER (1485—1555).
    On Christian Love 145

MELANCHTHON (1497—1560).
    The Safety of the Virtuous . . . 159

KNOX (1505—1572).
    The First Temptation of Christ . . 171

CALVIN (1509—1564).
    Enduring Persecution for Christ . . 203

BASIL

THE CREATION OF THE WORLD

BIOGRAPHICAL NOTE

BASIL, bishop of Cæsarea in Cappadocia, and styled "The Great," was the founder of Eastern monasticism, defender of the Nicene doctrines and doctor of the Church. He was born at Cæsarea in 329, and was thoroughly educated in all that a teacher like Libanius could impart at Rome, and Himerius at Constantinople. Returning home, he plunged into the pleasures of social life, but was induced by his sister to visit the hermits of Syria, Palestine and Egypt. Attracted during his travels to the religious life, he secluded himself in a lonely spot in inclement Pontus.

During his monastic life of seven years (357-364) he formulated the monastic rule still observed by Eastern monks. Ordained presbyter in 364, he labored in founding religious institutions of various kinds. He attracted notice by his growing Nicene predilections, and was elected bishop of his native town (370) and virtual primate of Asia Minor. His conduct in dealing with the Arians was uncompromising yet conciliating. As a theologian he stands next to his brother Gregory and to Athanasius, but he excels them both in the literary charm and variety of his Greek style. He died in 379.

BASIL
329—379

THE CREATION OF THE WORLD

The earth was without form and void.—Gen. i., 2.

IN the few words which have occupied us this morning we have found such a depth of thought that we despair of penetrating farther. If such is the forecourt of the sanctuary, if the portico of the temple is so grand and magnificent, if the splendor of its beauty thus dazzles the eyes of the soul, what will be the holy of holies? Who will dare to try to gain access to the innermost shrine? Who will look into its secrets? To gaze into it is indeed forbidden us, and language is powerless to express what the mind conceives.

However, since there are rewards, and most desirable ones, reserved by the just Judge for the intention alone of doing good, do not let us hesitate to continue our researches. Altho we may not attain to the truth, if, with the help of the Spirit, we do not fall away from the meaning of Holy Scripture, we shall not deserve to be rejected, and with the help of grace, we shall contribute to the edification of the Church of God.

"The earth," says Holy Scripture, "was without form and void"—*i.e.*, invisible and unfinished. The heavens and the earth were created together. How, then, is it that the heavens are perfect whilst the earth is still unformed and incomplete? In one word, what was the unfinished condition of the earth and for what reason was it invisible? The fertility of the earth is its perfect finishing; growth of all kinds of plants, the upspringing of tall trees, both productive and unfruitful, flowers' sweet scents and fair colors, and all that which, a little later, at the voice of God came forth from the earth to beautify her, their universal mother.

As nothing of all this yet existed, Scripture is right in calling the earth "without form." We could also say of the heavens that they were still imperfect and had not received their natural adornment, since at that time they did not shine with the glory of the sun and of the moon, and were not crowned by the choirs of the stars. These bodies were not yet created. Thus you will not diverge from the truth in saying that the heavens also were "without form." The earth was invisible for two reasons: it may be because man, the spectator, did not yet exist, or because, being submerged under the waters which overflowed the surface, it could not be seen, since the waters had not yet been gathered together into their own places, where God afterward collected them and gave them the name of sea.

What is invisible? First of all, that which

our fleshly eye can not perceive—our mind, for example; then that which, visible in its nature, is hidden by some body which conceals it, like iron in the depths of the earth. It is in this sense that the earth, in that it was hidden under the waters, was still invisible. However, as light did not yet exist, and as the earth lay in darkness because of the obscurity of the air above it, it should not astonish us that for this reason Scripture calls it "invisible."

But the corrupters of the truth, who, incapable of submitting their reason to Holy Scripture, distort at will the meaning of the Holy Scriptures, pretend that these words mean matter. For it is matter, they say, which from its nature is without form and invisible—being by the conditions of its existence without quality and without form and figure. The Artificer submitting it to the working of His wisdom clothed it with a form, organized it, and thus gave being to the visible world.

If the matter is uncreated, it has a claim to the same honors as God, since it must be of equal rank with Him. Is this not the summit of wickedness that utter chaos, without quality, without form or shape, ugliness without configuration, to use their own expression, should enjoy the same prerogatives as He who is wisdom, power, and beauty itself, the Creator and the Demiurge of the universe enjoys? This is not all. If the matter is so great as to be capable of being acted on by the whole wisdom of God, it would in a way raise its hypostasis to an equality with the inaccessible power of God, since it would be able to measure by itself all the extent of the divine intelligence.

If it is insufficient for the operations of God, then we fall into a more absurd blasphemy, since we condemn God for not being able, on account of the want of matter, to finish His own works. The resourcelessness of human nature has deceived these reasoners. Each of our crafts is exercised upon some special matter—the art of the smith upon iron, that of the carpenter on wood. In all there is the subject, the form and the work which results from the form. Matter is taken from without—art gives the form—and the work is composed at the same time of form and of matter.

Such is the idea that they make for themselves of the divine work. The form of the world is due to the wisdom of the supreme Artificer; matter came to the Creator from without; and thus the world results from a double origin. It has received from outside its matter and its essence, and from God its form and figure. They thus come to deny that the mighty God has presided at the formation of the universe, and pretend that he has only brought a crowning contribution

BASIL

to a common work; that he has only contributed some small portion to the genesis of beings; they are incapable, from the debasement of their reasonings, of raising their glances to the height of truth. Here, below, arts are subsequent to matter—introduced into life by the indispensable need of them. Wool existed before weaving made it supply one of nature's imperfections. Wood existed before carpentering took possession of it, and transformed it each day to supply new wants and made us see all the advantages derived from it, giving the oar to the sailor, the winnowing-fan to the laborer, the lance to the soldier.

But God, before all those things which now attract our notice existed, after casting about in His mind and determining to bring into being that which had no being, imagined the world such as it ought to be, and created matter in harmony with the form which He wished to give it. He assigned to the heavens the nature adapted for the heavens, and gave to the earth an essence in accordance with its form. He formed, as he wished, fire, air, and water, and gave to each the essence which the object of its existence required.

Finally he welded all the diverse parts of the universe by links of indissoluble attachment and established between them so perfect a fellowship and harmony that the most distant, in spite of their distance, appeared united in one universal sympathy. Let those men, therefore, renounce their fabulous imaginations, who in spite of the weakness of their argument, pretend to measure a power as incomprehensible to man's reason as it is unutterable by man's voice.

God created the heavens and the earth, but not only one-half of each; He created all the heavens and all the earth, creating the essence with the form. For He is not an inventor of figures, but the Creator even of the essence of beings. Further, let them tell us how the efficient power of God could deal with the passive nature of matter, the latter furnishing the matter without form, the former possessing the science of the form without matter, both being in need of each other; the Creator in order to display his art, matter in order to cease to be without form and to receive a form. But let us stop here and return to our subject.

"The earth was invisible and unfinished." In saying "In the beginning God created the heavens and the earth" the sacred writer passed over many things in silence—water, air, fire, and the results from them, which, all forming in reality the true complement of the world, were, without doubt made at the same time as the universe. By this silence history wishes to train the activity of our intelligence, giving it a weak point for starting, to impel it to the discovery of the truth.

BASIL

Thus, we are told of the creation of water; but, as we are told that the earth was invisible, ask yourself what could have covered it and prevented it from being seen? Fire could not conceal it. Fire brightens all about it, and spreads light rather than darkness around. No more was it air that enveloped the earth. Air by nature is of little density and transparent. It receives all kinds of visible objects and transmits them to the spectators. Only one supposition remains: that which floated on the surface of the earth was water, the fluid essence which had not yet been confined to its own place.

Thus the earth was not only invisible; it was still incomplete. Even to-day excessive damp is a hindrance to the productiveness of the earth. The same cause at the same time prevents it from being seen and from being complete, for the proper and natural adornment of the earth is its completion: corn waving in the valleys, meadows green with grass and rich with many-colored flowers, fertile glades and hilltops shaded by forests. Of all this nothing was yet produced; the earth was in travail with it in virtue of the power that she had received from the Creator. But she was waiting for the appointed time and the divine order to bring forth.

"Darkness was upon the face of the deep." A new source for fables and most impious imaginations may be found by distorting the sense of these words at the will of one's fancies. By "darkness" these wicked men do not understand what is meant in reality—air not illumined, the shadow produced by the interposition of a body, or finally a place for some reason deprived of light. For them "darkness" is an evil power, or rather the personification of evil, having his origin in himself in opposition to, and in perpetual struggle with, the goodness of God. If God is light, they say, without any doubt the power which struggles against Him must be darkness, "darkness" not owing its existence to a foreign origin, but an evil existing by itself. "Darkness" is the enemy of souls, the primary cause of death, the adversary of virtue. The words of the prophet, they say in their error, show that it exists and that it does not proceed from God. From this what perverse and impious dogmas have been imagined! What grievous wolves, tearing the flock of the Lord, have sprung from these words to cast themselves upon souls! Is it not from hence that have come forth Marcions and Valentinuses and the detestable heresy of the Manicheans which you may, without going far wrong, call the putrid humor of the churches?

O man, why wander thus from the truth and imagine for thyself that which will cause thy perdition? The word is simple and within the comprehension of all. "The earth was

BASIL

invisible." Why? Because the "deep" was spread over its surface. What is "the deep?" A mass of water of extreme depth. But we know that we can see many bodies through clear and transparent water. How, then, was it that no part of the earth appeared through the water? Because the air which surrounded it was still without light and in darkness. The rays of the sun, penetrating the water, often allow us to see the pebbles which form the bed of the river, but in a dark night it is impossible for our glance to penetrate under the water. Thus, these words, "the earth was invisible," are explained by those that follow; "the deep" covered it and itself was in darkness. Thus the deep is not a multitude of hostile powers, as has been imagined; nor "darkness" an evil sovereign force in enmity with good. In reality two rival principles of equal power, if engaged without ceasing in a war of mutual attacks, will end in self-destruction.

But if one should gain the mastery it would completely annihilate the conquered. Thus, to maintain the balance in the struggle between good and evil is to represent them as engaged in a war without end and in perpetual destruction, where the opponents are at the same time conquerors and conquered. If good is the stronger, what is there to prevent evil from being completely annihilated? But if that be the case, the very utterance of which is impious, I ask myself how it is that they themselves are not filled with horror to think that they have imagined such abominable blasphemies.

It is equally impious to say that evil has its origin from God; because the contrary can not proceed from its contrary. Life does not engender death; darkness is not the origin of light; sickness is not the maker of health. In the changes of conditions there are transitions from one condition to the contrary; but in genesis each being proceeds from its like and from its contrary. If, then, evil is neither uncreated nor created by God, from whence comes its nature? Certainly, that evil exists no one living in the world will deny. What shall we say, then? Evil is not a living animated essence: it is the condition of the soul opposed to virtue, developed in the careless on account of their falling away from good.

Do not, then, go beyond yourself to seek for evil, and imagine that there is an original nature of wickedness. Each of us—let us acknowledge it—is the first author of his own vice.

Among the ordinary events of life, some come naturally, like old age and sickness; others by chance, like unforeseen occurrences, of which the origin is beyond ourselves, often sad, sometimes fortunate—as, for instance, the discovery of a treasure when digging a well,

BASIL

or the meeting of a mad dog when going to the market-place.

Others depend upon ourselves; such as ruling one's passions, or not putting a bridle on one's pleasures; the mastery of anger, or resistance against him who irritates us; truth-telling or lying, the maintenance of a sweet and well-regulated disposition, or of a mood fierce and swollen and exalted with pride. Here you are the master of your actions. Do not look for the guiding cause beyond yourself, but recognize that evil, rightly so called, has no other origin than our voluntary falls. If it were involuntary, and did not depend upon ourselves, the laws would not have so much terror for the guilty, and the tribunals would not be so pitiless when they condemn wretches according to the measure of their crimes.

But enough concerning evil rightly so called. Sickness, poverty, obscurity, death, finally all human afflictions, ought not to be ranked as evils, since we do not count among the greatest boons things which are their opposites. Among these afflictions some are the effect of nature, others have obviously been for many a source of advantage. Let us be silent for the moment about these metaphors and allegories, and, simply following without vain curiosity the words of Holy Scripture, let us take from darkness the idea which it gives us.

But reason asks, Was darkness created with the world? Is it older than light? Why, in spite of its inferiority, has it preceded it? Darkness, we reply, did not exist in essence; it is a condition produced in the air by the withdrawal of light. What, then, is that light which disappeared suddenly from the world so that darkness should cover the face of the deep? If anything had existed before the formation of this sensible and perishable world, no doubt we conclude it would have been in the light. The orders of angels, the heavenly hosts, all intellectual natures named or unnamed, all the ministering spirits, did not live in darkness, but enjoyed a condition fitted for them in light and spiritual joy.

No one will contradict this, least of all he who looks for celestial light as one of the rewards promised to virtue—the light which, as Solomon says, is always a light to the righteous, the light which made the apostle say, "Giving thanks unto the Father, which hath made us meet to be partakers of the inheritance of the saints in light." Finally, if the condemned are sent into outer darkness, evidently those who are made worthy of God's approval are at rest in heavenly light. When, then, according to the order of God, the heaven appeared, enveloping all that its circumference included, a vast and unbroken body separating outer things from those which it enclosed, it necessarily kept the space inside in darkness for want of communication with the outer light.

Three things are, indeed, needed to form a shadow: light, a body, a dark place. The shadow of heaven forms the darkness of the world. Understand, I pray you, what I mean, by a simple example—by raising for yourself at midday a tent of some compact and impenetrable material, you shut yourself up in sudden darkness. Suppose that original darkness was like this, not subsisting directly by itself, but resulting from some external causes. If it is said that it rested upon the deep, it is because the extremity of air naturally touches the surface of bodies; and as at that time the water covered everything, we are obliged to say that darkness was upon the face of the deep.

"And the Spirit of God moved upon the face of the waters?" Does this Spirit mean the diffusion of air? The sacred writer wishes to enumerate to you the elements of the world, to tell you that God created the heavens, the earth, water and air, and that the last was now diffused and in motion; or rather, that which is truer and confirmed by the authority of the ancients, by the Spirit of God he means the Holy Spirit. It is, as has been remarked, the special name, the name above all others that Scripture delights to give to the Holy Spirit, and by the Spirit of God the Holy

Spirit is meant, the Spirit, namely, which completes the divine and blessed Trinity. You will always find it better, therefore, to take it in this sense. How, then, did the Spirit of God move upon the waters? The explanation that I am about to give you is not an original one, but that of a Syrian who was as ignorant in the wisdom of this world as he was versed in the knowledge of the truth.

He said, then, that the Syriac word was more expressive, and that, being more analogous to the Hebrew term, it was a nearer approach to the Scriptural sense. This is the meaning of the word: by "moved" the Syrians, he says, understand brooded over. The Spirit cherished the nature of the waters as one sees a bird cover the eggs with her body and impart to them vital force from her own warmth. Such is, as nearly as possible, the meaning of these words—the Spirit moved: that is, prepared the nature of water to produce living beings: a sufficient proof for those who ask if the Holy Spirit took an active part in the creation of the world.

"And God said, Let there be light." The first word uttered by God created the nature of light; it made darkness vanish, dispelled gloom, illuminated the world, and gave to all being at the same time a sweet and gracious aspect. The heavens, until then enveloped in darkness, appeared with that beauty which they still present to our eyes.

BASIL

The air was lighted up, or rather made the light circulate mixed with its substance, and, distributing its splendor rapidly in every direction, so dispersed itself to its extreme limits. Up it sprang to the very ether and heaven. In an instant it lighted up the whole extent of the world, the north and the south, the east and the west. For the ether also is such a subtle substance and so transparent that it needs not the space of a moment for light to pass through it. Just as it carries our sight instantaneously to the object of vision, so without the least interval, with a rapidity that thought can not conceive, it receives these rays of light in its uttermost limits. With light the ether becomes more pleasing and the waters more limpid. These last, not content with receiving its splendor, return it by the reflection of light and in all directions send forth quivering flashes. The divine word gives every object a more cheerful and a more attractive appearance, just as when men pour in oil into the deep sea they make the place about them smooth. So, with a single word and in one instant the Creator of all things gave the boon of light to the world.

"Let there be light." The order was itself an operation, and a state of things was brought into being than which man's mind can not even imagine a pleasanter one for our enjoyment. It must be well understood that when we speak of the voice, of the word, of the command of God, this divine language does not mean to us a sound which escapes from the organs of speech, a collision of air struck by the tongue; it is a simple sign of the will of God, and, if we give it the form of an order, it is only the better to impress the souls whom we instruct.

"And God saw the light, that it was good." How can we worthily praise light after the testimony given by the Creator to its goodness? The word, even among us, refers the judgment to the eyes, incapable of raising itself to the idea that the senses have already received. But if beauty in bodies results from symmetry of parts and the harmonious appearance of colors how, in a simple and homogeneous essence like light, can this idea of beauty be preserved? Would not the symmetry in light be less shown in its parts than in the pleasure and delight at the sight of it? Such is also the beauty of gold, which it owes, not to the happy mingling of its parts, but only to its beautiful color, which has a charm attractive to the eyes.

Thus, again, the evening star is the most beautiful of the stars: not that the parts of which it is composed form a harmonious whole, but thanks to the unalloyed and beautiful brightness which meets our eyes. And further, when God proclaimed the goodness of light, it was not in regard to the charm of the eye, but as a provision for future advantage, because at that time there were as yet no eyes to judge of its beauty.

"And God divided the light from the darkness." That is to say, God gave them natures incapable of mixing, perpetually in opposition to each other, and put between them the widest space and distance.

"And God called the light day, and the darkness he called night." Since the birth of the sun, the light that it diffuses in the air when shining on our hemisphere is day, and the shadow produced by its disappearance is night. But at that time it was not after the movement of the sun, but following this primitive light spread abroad in the air or withdrawn in a measure determined by God, that day came and was followed by night.

"And the evening and the morning were the first day." Evening is then the boundary common to day and night; and in the same way morning constitutes the approach of night to day. It was to give day the privileges of seniority that Scripture put the end of the first day before that of the first night, because night follows day: for, before the creation of light, the world was not in night, but in darkness. It is the opposite of day which was called night, and it did not receive its name until after day. Thus were created the evening and the morning. Scripture means the space of a day and a night, and afterward no more says day and night, but calls them both under the name of the more important: a custom which you will find throughout Scripture. Everywhere the measure of time is counted by days without mention of nights. "The days of our years," says the Psalmist; "few and evil have the days of the years of my life been," said Jacob; and elsewhere "all the days of my life."

"And the evening and the morning were the first day," or, rather, one day.—(*Revised Vers*). Why does Scripture say "one day," not "the first day?" Before speaking to us of the second, the third, and the fourth days, would it not have been more natural to call that one the first which began the series? If it, therefore, says "one day," it is from a wish to determine the measure of day and night and to combine the time that they contain. Now, twenty-four hours fill up the space of one day—we mean of a day and of a night; and if, at the time of the solstices, they have not both an equal length, the time marked by Scripture does not the less circumscribe their duration. It is as tho it said: Twenty-four hours measure the space of a day, or a day is in reality the time that the heavens, starting from one point, take to return thither. Thus, every time that, in the revolution of the sun, evening and morning occupy the world, their periodical succession never exceeds the space of one day.

But we must believe that there is a mysterious reason for this? God, who made the nature of time, measured it out and determined it by intervals of days; and, wishing to give it a week as a measure, he ordered the week to resolve from period to period upon itself, to count the movement of time, forming the week of one day revolving seven times upon itself: a proper circle begins and ends with itself. Such is also the character of eternity, to revolve upon itself and to end nowhere. If, then, the beginning of time is called "one day" rather than "the first day," it is because Scripture wishes to establish its relationship with eternity. It was, in reality, fit and natural to call "one" the day whose character is to be one wholly separated and isolated from all others. If Scripture speaks to us of many ages, saying everywhere "age of age, and ages of ages," we do not see it enumerate them as first, second, and third. It follows that we are hereby shown, not so much limits, ends, and succession of ages as distinctions between various states and modes of action. "The day of the Lord," Scripture says, "is great and very terrible," and elsewhere, "Woe unto you that desire the day of the Lord: to what end is it for you? The day of the Lord is darkness and not light."

A day of darkness for those who are worthy of darkness. No; this day without evening, without succession, and without end is not unknown to Scripture, and it is the day that the Psalmist calls the eighth day, because it is outside this time of weeks. Thus, whether you call it day or whether you call it eternity, you express the same idea. Give this state the name of day; there are not several, but only one. If you call it eternity still it is unique and not manifold. Thus it is in order that you may carry your thoughts forward toward a future life that Scripture marks by the word "one" the day which is the type of eternity, the first-fruits of days, the contemporary of light, the holy Lord's day.

But while I am conversing with you about the first evening of the world, evening takes me by surprize and puts an end to my discourse. May the Father of the true light, who has adorned day with celestial light, who has made to shine the fires which illuminate us during the night, who reserves for us in the peace of a future age a spiritual and everlasting light, enlighten your hearts in the knowledge of truth, keep you from stumbling, and grant that "you may walk honestly as in the day." Thus shall you shine as the sun in the midst of the glory of the saints, and I shall glory in you in the day of Christ, to whom belong all glory and power for ever and ever. Amen.

CHRYSOSTOM

EXCESSIVE GRIEF AT THE DEATH OF FRIENDS

BIOGRAPHICAL NOTE

CHRYSOSTOM (that is, "Of the Golden Mouth") was a title given to John, Archbishop of Constantinople. He was born of a patrician family at Antioch about 347, and owed much to the early Christian training of his Christian mother, Anthusa. He studied under Libanius, and for a time practised law, but was converted and baptized in 368. He made a profound study of the Scriptures, the whole of which, it is said, he learned to repeat by heart.

Like Basil and Gregory he began his religious life as a hermit in the desert. After six years he returned to Antioch, where he gained reputation as the greatest preacher in the Eastern Church. Raised to the metropolitan See of Constantinople in 397, his fulminations against the corruptions of the court caused him to be banished, after a stormy ministry of six years. He was recalled in response to popular clamor, but removed again, and shortly after died, in 407. He was a great exegete, and showed a spirit of intellectual liberty which anticipated modern criticism. Sermons to the number of one thousand have been attributed to him.

CHRYSOSTOM
347—407

EXCESSIVE GRIEF AT THE DEATH OF FRIENDS

But I would not have you to be ignorant, brethren, concerning them which are asleep, that ye sorrow not.
—1 Thess. iv., 13.

WE have occupied four days in explaining to you the parable of Lazarus, bringing out the treasure that we found in a body covered with sores; a treasure, not of gold and silver and precious stones, but of wisdom and fortitude, of patience and endurance. For as in regard to visible treasures, while the surface of the ground shows only thorns and briers, and rough earth, yet, let a person dig deep into it, abundant wealth discovers itself; so it has proved in respect to Lazarus. Outwardly, wounds; but underneath these, unspeakable wealth; a body pining away, but a spirit noble and wakeful. We have also seen an illustration of that remark of the apostle's—in proportion as the outward man perishes, the inward man is renewed.

It would, indeed, be proper to address you to-day, also, on this same parable, and to enter the lists with those heretics who censure the Old Testament, bringing accusations against the patriarchs, and whetting their tongues against God, the Creator of the universe. But to avoid wearying you and reserving this controversy for another time, let us direct the discourse to another subject; for a table with only one sort of food produces satiety, while variety provokes the appetite. That it may be so in regard to our preaching, let us now, after a long period, turn to the blest Paul; for very opportunely has a passage from the apostle been read to-day, and the things which are to be spoken concerning it are in harmony with those that have lately been presented. Hear, then, Paul this day proclaiming—"I would not have you to be ignorant concerning them which are asleep, that ye sorrow not even as others which have no hope." The parable of Lazarus is the evangelical chord; this passage is the apostolic note. And there is concord between them; for we have, on that parable, said much concerning the resurrection and the future judgment, and our discourse now recurs to that theme; so that, tho it is on apostolic ground we are now toiling, we shall here find the same treasure. For in treating the parable, our aim was to teach the hearers this lesson, that they should regard all the splendors of the present life as nothing, but should look forward in their hopes, and daily reflect on the decisions which will be hereafter pronounced, and on that fearful judgment, and that Judge who can not be deceived. On these things Paul has counseled us to-day in the passages which have been read to us. Attend, however, to his own words—"I would not have you to be ignorant, brethren, concerning them which are asleep, that ye sorrow not, even as others which have no hope. For if we believe that Jesus died and rose again, even so them also which sleep in Jesus will God bring with him."—I Thess. iv., 13, 14.

We ought here, at the outset, to inquire why, when he is speaking concerning Christ, he employs the word death; but when he is speaking of our decease he calls it sleep, and not death. For he did not say, Concerning them that are dead: but what did he say? "Concerning them that are asleep." And again—"Even so them also which sleep in Jesus will God bring with Him." He did not say, Them that have died. Still again—"We who are alive and remain unto the coming of the Lord shall not prevent them that sleep." Here, too, he did not say—Them that are dead; but a third time, bringing the subject to their remembrance, for the third time called death a sleep. Concerning Christ, however, he did not speak thus; but how? "For if we believe that Jesus died." He did not say, Jesus slept, but He died. Why now did he use the term death in reference to Christ, but in reference to us the term sleep? For it was not casually, or negligently, that he employed this expression, but he had a wise and great purpose in so doing. In speaking of Christ, he said death, so as to confirm the fact that Christ had actually suffered death; in speaking of us, he said sleep, in order to impart consolation. For where resurrection had already taken place, he mentions death with plainness; but where the resurrection is still a matter of hope, he says sleep, consoling us by this very expression, and cherishing our valuable hopes. For he who is only asleep will surely awake; and death is no more than a long sleep.

Say not a dead man hears not, nor speaks, nor sees, nor is conscious. It is just so with a sleeping person. If I may speak somewhat paradoxically, even the soul of a sleeping person is in some sort asleep; but not so the soul of a dead man; that is awake.

But, you say, a dead man experiences corruption, and becomes dust and ashes. And what then, beloved hearers? For this very reason we ought to rejoice. For when a man is about to rebuild an old and tottering house, he first sends out its occupants, then tears it down, and rebuilds anew a more splendid one. This occasions no grief to the occupants, but rather joy; for they do not think of the demolition which they see, but of the house which is to come, tho not yet seen. When God is about to do a similar work, he destroys our body, and removes the soul which was dwelling in it as from some house, that he may build it anew and more splendidly, and again bring the soul into it with greater glory. Let us not, therefore, regard the tearing down, but the splendor which is to succeed.

If, again, a man has a statue decayed by rust and age, and mutilated in many of its parts, he breaks it up and casts it into a furnace, and after the melting he receives it again in a more beautiful form. As then the dissolving in the furnace was not a destruction but a renewing of the statue, so the death of our bodies is not a destruction but a renovation. When, therefore, you see as in a furnace our flesh flowing away to corruption, dwell not on that sight, but wait for the recasting. And be not satisfied with the extent of this illustration, but advance in your thoughts to a still higher point; for the statuary, casting into the furnace a brazen image, does not furnish you in its place a golden and undecaying statue, but again makes a brazen one. God does not thus; but casting in a mortal body formed of clay, he returns to you a golden and immortal statue; for the earth, receiving a corruptible and decaying body gives back the same, incorruptible and undecaying. Look not, therefore, on the corpse, lying with closed eyes and speechless lips, but on the man that is risen, that has received glory unspeakable and amazing, and direct your thoughts from the present sight to the future hope.

But do you miss his society, and therefore lament and mourn? Now is it not unreasonable, that, if you should have given your daughter in marriage, and her husband should take her to a distant country and should there enjoy prosperity, you would not think the circumstance a calamity, but the intelligence of their prosperity would console the sorrow occasioned by her absence; and yet here, while it is not a man, nor a fellow servant, but the Lord Himself who has taken your relative, that you should grieve and lament?

And how is it possible, you ask, not to grieve, since I am only a man? Nor do I say that you should not grieve: I do not condemn dejection, but the intensity of it. To be dejected is natural; but to be overcome by dejection is madness, and folly, and unmanly weakness. You may grieve and weep; but give not way to despondency, nor indulge in complaints. Give thanks to God, who has taken your friend, that you have the opportunity of honoring the departed one, and of dismissing him with becoming obsequies. If you sink under depression, you withhold honor from the departed, you displease God who has taken him, and you injure yourself;

but if you are grateful, you pay respect to him, you glorify God, and you benefit yourself. Weep, as wept your Master over Lazarus, observing the just limits of sorrow, which it is not proper to pass. Thus also said Paul—"I would not have you to be ignorant concerning them which are asleep, that ye sorrow not as others who have no hope. Grieve," says he; "but not as the Greek, who has no hope of a resurrection, who despairs of a future life."

Believe me, I am ashamed and blush to see unbecoming groups of women pass along the mart, tearing their hair, cutting their arms and cheeks—and all this under the eyes of the Greeks. For what will they not say? What will they not declare concerning us? Are these the men who reason about a resurrection? Indeed! How poorly their actions agree with their opinions! In words, they reason about a resurrection: but they act just like those who do not acknowledge a resurrection. If they fully believed in a resurrection, they would not act thus; if they had really persuaded themselves that a deceased friend had departed to a better state, they would not thus mourn. These things, and more than these, the unbelievers say when they hear those lamentations. Let us then be ashamed, and be more moderate, and not occasion so much harm to ourselves and to those who are looking on us.

For on what account, tell me, do you thus weep for one departed? Because he was a bad man? You ought on that very account to be thankful, since the occasions of wickedness are now cut off. Because he was good and kind? If so, you ought to rejoice; since he has been soon removed, before wickedness had corrupted him, and he has gone away to a world where he stands even secure, and there is no reason even to mistrust a change. Because he was a youth? For that, too, praise Him that has taken him, because he has speedily called him to a better lot. Because he was an aged man? On this account, also, give thanks and glorify Him that has taken him. Be ashamed of your behavior at a burial. The singing of psalms, the prayers, the assembling of the (spiritual) fathers and brethren—all this is not that you may weep, and lament, and afflict yourselves, but that you may render thanks to Him who has taken the departed. For as when men are called to some high office, multitudes with praises on their lips assemble to escort them at their departure to their stations, so do all with abundant praise join to send forward, as to greater honor, those of the pious who have departed. Death is rest, a deliverance from the exhausting labors and cares of this world. When, then, thou seest a relative departing, yield not to despondency; give thyself to reflection; examine thy conscience;

cherish the thought that after a little while this end awaits thee also. Be more considerate; let another's death excite thee to salutary fear; shake off all indolence; examine your past deeds; quit your sins, and commence a happy change.

We differ from unbelievers in our estimate of things. The unbeliever surveys the heavens and worships them, because he thinks them a divinity; he looks to the earth and makes himself a servant to it, and longs for the things of sense. But not so with us. We survey the heavens and admire Him that made them; for we do not believe them to be a god, but a work of God. I look on the whole creation, and am led by it to the Creator. He looks on wealth, and longs for it with earnest desire; I look on wealth, and contemn it. He sees poverty, and laments; I see poverty, and rejoice. I see things in one light; he in another. Just so in regard to death. He sees a corpse, and thinks of it as a corpse; I see a corpse, and behold sleep rather than death. And as in regard to books, both learned persons and unlearned see them with the same eyes, but not with the same understanding—for to the unlearned the mere shapes of letters appear, while the learned discover the sense that lies within those letters—so in respect to affairs in general, we all see what takes place with the same eyes, but not with the same understanding and judgment. Since, therefore, in all other things we differ from them, shall we agree with them in our sentiments respecting death?

Consider to whom the departed has gone, and take comfort. He has gone where Paul is, and Peter, and the whole company of the saints. Consider how he shall arise, with what glory and splendor. Consider that by mourning and lamenting thou canst not alter the event which has occurred, and thou wilt in the end injure thyself. Consider whom you imitate by so doing, and shun this companionship in sin. For whom do you imitate and emulate? The unbelieving, those who have no hope; as Paul has said—"That ye sorrow not, even as others who have no hope." And observe how carefully he expresses himself; for he does not say, Those who have not the hope of a resurrection, but simply, Those who have no hope. He that has no hope of a future retribution has no hope at all, nor does he know that there is a God, nor that God exercises a providential care over present occurrences, nor that divine justice looks on all things. But he that is thus ignorant and inconsiderate is more unwise than a beast, and separates his soul from all good; for he that does not expect to render an account of his deeds cuts himself loose from all virtue, and attaches himself to all vice. Considering these things, therefore, and reflecting on the folly and stupidity of the heathen, whose associates we become by our lamentations for the dead, let us avoid this conformity to them. For the apostle mentions them for this very purpose, that by considering the dishonor into which thou fallest, thou mightest recover thyself from this conformity, and return to thy proper dignity.

And not only here, but everywhere and frequently, the blest Paul does the same. For when he would dissuade from sin, he shows with whom we become associated by our sins, that, being touched by the character of the persons, thou shouldest avoid such companionship. To the Thessalonians, accordingly, he says, Let every one "possess his vessel in sanctification and honor, not in the lust of concupiscence, even as the Gentiles which know not God." And again—"Walk not as the other Gentiles in the vanity of their mind." Thus also here—"I would not have you to be ignorant, brethren, concerning them which are asleep, that ye sorrow not even as others who have no hope." For it is not the nature of things, but our own disposition, which makes us grieve; not the death of the departed, but the weakness of those who mourn.

We ought, therefore, to thank God not only for the resurrection, but also for the hope of it; which can comfort the afflicted soul, and bid us be of good cheer concerning the departed, for they will again rise and be with us. If we must have anguish, we should mourn and lament over those who are living in sin, not over those who have died righteously. Thus did Paul; for he says to the Corinthians—"Lest when I come to you God shall humble me among you and that I shall bewail many." He was not speaking of those who had died, but of those who had sinned and had not repented of the lasciviousness and uncleanness which they had committed; over these it was proper to mourn. So likewise another writer admonishes, saying—"Weep over the dead, for the light has failed; and weep over the fool, for understanding has failed" (Eccles. xxii., 10). Weep a little for the dead; for he has gone to his rest; but the fool's life is a greater calamity than death. And surely if one devoid of understanding is always a proper object of lamentation, much more he that is devoid of righteousness and that has fallen from hope toward God. These, then, let us bewail; for such bewailing may be useful. For often while lamenting these, we amend our own faults; but to bewail the departed is senseless and hurtful. Let us not, then, reverse the order, but bewail only sin; and all other things, whether poverty, or sickness, or untimely death, or calumny, or false accusation, or whatever human evil befalls us, let us resolutely bear them all. For these calamities, if we are watchful, will be the occasions of adding to our crowns.

But how is it possible, you ask, that a bereaved person, being a man, should not grieve? On the contrary, I ask, how is it that being a man he should grieve, since he is honored with reason and with hopes of future good? Who is there, you ask again, that has not been subdued by this weakness? Many, I reply, and in many places, both among us and among those who have died before us. Job, for instance; the whole circle of his children being taken away, hear what he says —"The Lord gave; the Lord hath taken away; blessed be the name of the Lord." A wonderful saying, even when merely heard; but if you examine it closely, your wonder will greatly increase.

For consider; Satan did not take merely half and leave half, or take the larger number and leave the rest; but he gathered all the fruit, and yet did not prevail in uprooting the tree; he covered the whole sea with waves, and yet did not overwhelm the bark; he despoiled the tower of its strength, and yet could not batter it down. Job stood firm, tho assailed from every quarter; showers of arrows fell, but they did not wound him. Consider how great a thing it was, to see so many children perish. Was it not enough to pierce him to the quick that they should all be snatched away?—altogether and in one day; in the flower of life; having shown so much virtue; expiring as by a stroke of vengeance; that after so many sorrows this last should be inflicted; that the father was fond of them, and that the deceased were worthy of his affection. When a man loses vicious children, he does indeed suffer grief, but not intense grief; for the wickedness of the departed does not allow the sorrow to be poignant. But when children are virtuous, an abiding wound is inflicted, the remembrance is indelible, the calamity is inconsolable; there is a double sting, from nature, and from the virtuous character of the departed.

That Job's children were virtuous, appears from the fact that their father was particularly solicitous in regard to them, and rising up offered sacrifices in their behalf, fearing lest they might have committed secret sins; and no consideration was more important in his esteem than this. Not only the virtue of the children is thus shown, but also the affectionate spirit of the father. Since, therefore, the father was so affectionate, showing not only a love for them which proceeded from nature, but that also which came from their piety, and since the departed were thus virtuous, the anguish had a threefold intensity. Still further; when children are torn away separately, the suffering has some consolation; for those that are left alleviate the sorrow over the departed; but when the whole circle is gone, to what one of all his numerous children can the childless man now look?

Besides these causes of sorrow, there was a fifth stroke. What was that? That they were all snatched away at once. For if in the case of those who die after three or five days of sickness, the women and all the relatives bewail this most of all, that the deceased was taken away from their sight speedily and suddenly, much more might he have been distrest, when thus deprived of all, not in three days, or two, or one, but in one hour! For a calamity long contemplated, even if it be hard to bear, may fall more lightly through this anticipation; but that which happens contrary to expectation and suddenly is intolerable.

Would you hear of a sixth stroke? He lost them all in the very flower of their age. You know how very overwhelming are untimely bereavements, and productive of grief on many scores. The instance we are contemplating was not only untimely, but also violent; so that here was a seventh stroke. For their father did not see them expire on a bed, but they are all overwhelmed by the falling habitation. Consider then; a man was digging in that pile of ruins, and now he drew up a stone, and now a limb of a deceased one; he saw a hand still holding a cup, and another right hand placed on the table, and the mutilated form of a body, the nose torn away, the head crusht, the eyes put out, the brain scattered, the whole frame marred, and the variety of wounds not permitting the father to recognize the beloved countenances. You suffer emotions and shed tears at merely hearing of these things: what must he have endured at the sight of them? For if we, so long after the event, can not bear to hear of this tragedy, tho it was another man's calamity, what an adamant was he to look on these things, and contemplate them, not as another's, but his own afflictions! He did not give way to dejection, nor ask, "What does this mean? Is this the recompense for my kindness? Was it for this that I opened my house, that I might see it made the grave of my children? Did I for this exhibit every parental virtue, that they should endure such a death?" No such things did he speak, or even think; but steadily bore all, tho bereaved of them after bestowing on them so much care. For as an accomplished statuary framing golden images adorns them with great care, so he sought properly to mold and adorn their souls. And as a husbandman assiduously waters his palm-trees, or olives, inclosing them and cultivating them in every suitable way; so he perpetually sought to enrich each one's soul, as a fruitful olive, with increasing virtue. But he saw the trees overthrown by the assault of the evil spirit, and exposed on the earth, and enduring that miserable kind of death; yet he uttered no reviling word, but rather blest God, thus giving a deadly blow to the devil.

Should you say that Job had many sons, but that others have frequently lost their only sons, and that his cause of sorrow was not equal to theirs, you say well; but I reply, that Job's cause of sorrow was not only equal, but far greater. For of what advantage was it to him that he had many children? It was a severer calamity and a more bitter grief to receive the wound in many bodies.

Still, if you wish to see another holy man having an only son, and showing the same and even greater fortitude, call to mind the patriarch Abraham, who did not indeed see Isaac die, but, what was much more painful, was himself commanded to slay him, and did not question the command, nor repine at it, nor say, "Is it for this thou hast made me a father, that thou shouldest make me the slayer of my son? Better it would have been not to give him at all, than having given him thus to take him away. And if thou choosest to take him, why dost thou command me to slay him and to pollute my right hand? Didst thou not promise me that from this son thou wouldst fill the earth with my descendants? How wilt thou give the fruits, then, if thou pluck up the root? How dost thou promise me a posterity, and yet order me to slay my son? Who ever saw such things, or heard of the like? I am deceived; I have been deluded." No such thing did he say, or even think; he said nothing against the command, he did not ask the reasons; but hearing the Word—"Take thy son, thine only son whom thou lovest, and carry him up to one of the mountains which I shall show thee," he complied so readily as even to do more than was commanded. For he concealed the matter from his wife, and he left the servants at the foot of the Mount in ignorance of what was to be done, and ascended, taking only the victim. Thus not unwillingly, but with promptness, he obeyed the command. Think now what it was, to be conversing alone with his son, apart from all others, when the affections are the more fervently excited, and attachment becomes stronger; and this not for one, or two, but for several days. To obey the command speedily would have been wonderful; but not so wonderful as, while his heart was burdened and agitated for many days, to avoid indulging in human tenderness toward his son. On this account God appointed for him a more extended arena, and a longer race-course, that thou mightest the more carefully observe his combatant. A combatant he was indeed, contending not against a man, but against the force of nature. What language can describe his fortitude? He brought forward his son, bound him, placed him on the wood, seized the sacrificial knife, was just on the point of dealing the stroke. In what manner to express myself properly, I know not; he only would know, who did these things. For no language can describe how it happened that his hand did not become torpid, that the strength of his nerves did not relax, that the affecting sight of his son did not overpower him.

It is proper here, too, to admire Isaac. For as the one obeyed God, so did the other obey his father; and as the one, at God's bidding him to sacrifice, did not demand an account of the matter, so the other, when his father was binding him and leading him to the altar, did not say, "Why art thou doing this?"—but surrendered himself to his father's hand. And then was to be seen a man uniting in his own person the father and the sacrificing priest; and a sacrifice offered without blood, a whole burnt offering without fire, an altar representing a type of death and the resurrection. For he both sacrificed his son and he did not sacrifice him. He did not sacrifice him with his hand, but in his purpose. For God gave the command, not through desire to see the flowing of the blood, but to give you a specimen of steady purpose, to make known throughout the world this worthy man, and to instruct all in coming time that it is necessary to prefer the command of God before children and nature, before all things, and even life itself. And so Abraham descended from the Mount, bringing alive the martyr Isaac. How can we be pardoned then, tell me, or what apology can we have, if we see that noble man obeying God with so much promptness and submitting to Him in all things, and yet we murmur at His dispensations? Tell me not of grief, nor of the intolerable nature of your calamity; rather consider how in the midst of bitter sorrow you may yet rise superior to it. That which was commanded to Abraham was enough to stagger his reason, to throw him into perplexity, and to undermine his faith in the past. For who would not have then thought that the promise which had been made him of a numerous posterity was all a deception? But not so Abraham. And not less ought we to admire Job's wisdom in calamity; and particularly, that after so much virtue, after his alms and various acts of kindness to men, and tho aware of no wrong either in himself or his children, yet experiencing so much affliction, affliction so singular, such as had never happened even to the most desperately wicked, still he was not affected by it as most men would have been, nor did he regard his virtue as profitless, nor form any ill-advised opinion concerning the past.

By these two examples, then, we ought not only to admire virtue, but to emulate and imitate it. And let no one say these were wonderful men. True, they were wonderful and great men. But we are now required to have more wisdom than they, and than all who lived under the Old Testament. For "except your righteousness exceed that of the Scribes and Pharisees, ye shall not enter into the kingdom of heaven." Gathering wisdom, then, from all quarters, and considering what we are told concerning a resurrection and concerning these holy men, let us frequently recite it to our souls, not only when we are actually in sorrow, but also while we are free from distress. For I have now address you on this subject, tho no one is in particular affliction, that when we shall fall into any such calamity, we may, from the remembrance of what has been said, obtain requisite consolation. As soldiers, even in peace, perform warlike exercises, so that when actually called to battle and the occasion makes a demand for skill, they may avail themselves of the art which they have cultivated in peace; so let us, in time of peace, furnish ourselves with weapons and remedies, that whenever there shall burst on us a war of unreasonable passions, or grief, or pain, or any such thing, we may, well armed and secure on all sides, repel the assaults of the evil one with all skill, and wall ourselves round with right contemplations, with the declarations of God, with the examples of good men, and with every possible defense. For so shall we be able to pass the present life with happiness, and to attain to the kingdom of heaven, through Jesus Christ, to whom be glory and dominion, together with the Father and the Holy Spirit, forever and ever. Amen.

AUGUSTINE

THE RECOVERY OF SIGHT BY THE BLIND

BIOGRAPHICAL NOTE

SAINT AUGUSTINE (Aurelius Augustinus), one of the greatest theological fathers of the Church, was born at Tagaste, 354 A.D., and became devoted to the study of Cicero. As a Manichean he occasioned great anxiety to his mother Monica. Eventually embracing Christianity, he was baptized by Ambrose of Milan (387), on which occasion, tradition says, the Te Deum was composed by himself and his baptizer. Appointed to the See of Hippo in 395, he threw himself into the conflict against heresy and schism, his principal opponents being the Donatists and Pelagians. His sermons, powerful as they are, disappoint the modern reader by their fantastic and allegorical interpretation of Scripture, but his "Confessions," in which he details the history of his early life and conversion, present a wonderful picture of personal experience. He is styled by Harnack "the first modern man." He died at Hippo in 430.

AUGUSTINE
354—430

THE RECOVERY OF SIGHT BY THE BLIND

Have mercy on us, O Lord, thou son of David.—
Matt. xx., 30.

I. YE know, holy brethren, full well as we do, that our Lord and Savior Jesus Christ is the physician of our eternal health; and that to this end we task the weakness of our natures, that our weakness might not last forever. For He assumed a mortal body, wherein to kill death. And, "though He was crucified through weakness," as the apostle saith, yet He "liveth by the power of God." They are the words, too, of the same apostle: "He dieth no more, death hath no more dominion over Him." These things, I say, are well known to your faith. And there is also this which follows from them, that we should know that all the miracles which He did on the body avail to our instruction, that we may from them perceive that which is not to pass away, nor to have any end. He restored to the blind those eyes which death was sure some time to close; He raised Lazarus to life who was to die again. And whatever He did for the health of bodies, He did it not to this end that they should be forever; whereas, at the last, He will give eternal health even to the body itself. But because those things which were not seen were not believed; by means of those temporal things which were seen, He built up faith in those things which were not seen.

II. Let no one then, brethren, say that our Lord Jesus Christ doeth not those things now, and on this account prefer the former to the present ages of the Church. In a certain place, indeed, the same Lord prefers those who do not see and yet believe to them who see and therefore believe. For even at that time so irresolute was the infirmity of His disciples that they thought that He whom they saw to have risen again must be handled, in order that they might believe. It was not enough for their eyes that they had seen Him, unless their hands also were applied to His limbs, and the scars of His recent wounds were touched: that this disciple, who was in doubt, might cry suddenly when he had touched and recognized the scars, "My Lord and my God." The scars manifested Him who had healed all wounds in others. Could not the Lord have risen again without scars? Yes, but He knew the wounds which were in the hearts of His disciples, and to heal them He had preserved the scars on His own body. And what said the Lord to him who now confest and said, "My lord, and my God?" "Because thou hast seen," He said, "thou hast believed; blessed are they who have not seen, and yet have believed." Of whom spake He, brethren, but of us? Not that He spoke only of us, but of those also who shall come after us. For a little while when He had departed from the sight of men, that faith might be established in their hearts, whosoever believed, believed tho they saw Him not, and great has been the merit of their faith; for the procuring of which faith they brought only the movement of a pious heart, and not the touching of their hands.

III. These things, then, the Lord did to invite us to the faith. This faith reigneth now in the Church, which is spread throughout the whole world. And now, He worketh greater cures, on account of which He disdained not then to exhibit those lesser ones. For as the soul is better than the body, so is the saving health of the soul better than the health of the body. The blind body doth not now open its eyes by a miracle of the Lord, but the blinded heart openeth its eyes to the word of the Lord. The mortal corpse doth not now rise again, but the soul doth rise again which lay dead in a living body. The deaf ears of the body are not now opened; but how many have the ears of their heart closed, which yet fly open at the penetrating word of God, so that they believe who did not believe, and they live well who did live evilly, and they obey who did not obey; and we say, "such a man is become a believer," and we wonder when we hear of them whom once we had known as hardened. Why, then, dost thou marvel at one who now believes, who is living innocently, and serving God, but because thou dost behold him seeing, whom thou hadst known to be blind; dost behold him living whom thou hast known to be dead; dost behold him hearing whom thou hadst known to be deaf? For consider that there are those who are dead in another than the ordinary sense, of whom the Lord spoke to a certain man who delayed to follow the Lord, because he wished to bury his father; "Let the dead," said He, "bury their dead." Surely these dead buriers are not dead in body; for if this were so, they could not bury dead bodies. Yet doth He call them dead; where but in the soul within? For as we may often see in a household, itself sound and well, the master of the same house lying dead; so in a sound body do many carry a dead soul within; and these the apostle arouses thus, "Awake, thou that sleepest, and arise from the dead, and Christ shall give thee light." It is the same who giveth sight to the blind that awakeneth the dead. For it is with His voice that the cry is made by the apostle to the dead. "Awake thou that sleepest." And the blind will be enlightened with light, when he shall have risen again. And how many deaf men did the Lord see before His eyes, when He said, "He that hath ears to hear let him hear." For who was standing before Him without his bodily ears? What other ears, then, did He seek for, but those of the inner man?

IV. Again, what eyes did He look for when He spake to those who saw indeed, but who saw only with the eyes of the flesh? For when Philip said to Him, "Lord, show us the Father and it sufficeth us": he understood, indeed, that if the Father were shown him, it might well suffice him; when He that was equal to the Father had sufficed not? And why did He not suffice? Because He was not seen. And why was He not seen? Because the eye whereby He might be seen was not yet whole. For this, namely, that the Lord was seen in the flesh with the outward eyes, not only the disciples who honored Him saw, but also the Jews who crucified Him. He, then, who wished to be seen in another way, sought for other eyes. And, therefore, it was that to him who said, "Show us the Father, and it sufficeth us," He answered, "Have I been so long time with you, and yet hast thou not known Me, Philip? He who hath seen Me hath seen the Father also." And that He might in the meanwhile heal the eyes of faith, He has first of all given him instructions regarding faith, that so he might attain to sight. And lest Philip should think that he was to conceive of God under the same form in which he then saw the Lord Jesus Christ in the body, he immediately subjoined, "Believest thou not that I am in the Father, and the Father in me?" He had already said, "He who hath seen me hath seen the Father also." But Philip's eye was not yet sound enough to see the Father, nor, consequently, to see the Son, who is Himself coequal with the Father. And so Jesus Christ took in hand to cure, and with the medicine and salve of faith to strengthen the eyes of his mind, which as yet were weak and unable to behold so great a light, and He said, "Believest thou not that I am in the Father, and the Father in Me?" Let not him, then, who can not yet see what the Lord will one day show him, seek first to see what he is to believe; but let him first believe that the eye by which he is to see may be healed. For it was only the form of the servant which was exhibited to the eyes of servants; because if "He who thought it not robbery to be equal with God" could have been now seen as equal with God by those whom He wished to be healed, He would not have needed to empty Himself and to take the form of a servant. But because there was no way whereby God could be seen, but whereby man could be seen there was;

therefore, He who was God was made man, that that which was seen might heal that whereby He was not seen. For He saith Himself in another place, "Blessed are the pure in heart, for they shall see God." Philip might, of course, have answered and said, Lord, do I see Thee? Is the Father such as I see Thee to be? Forasmuch as Thou hast said, "He who hath seen Me hath seen the Father also?" But before Philip answered thus, or perhaps before he so much as thought it, when the Lord had said, "He who hath seen Me hath seen the Father also," He immediately added, "Believest thou not that I am in the Father, and the Father in me?" For with that eye he could not yet see either the Father, or the Son who is equal with the Father; but that his eye might be healed for seeing, he was anointed unto believing. So, then, before thou seest what thou canst not now see, believe what as yet thou seest not. "Walk by faith," that thou mayest attain to sight. Sight will not gladden him in his home whom faith consoleth not by the way. For, so says the apostle, "As long as we are in the body we are absent from the Lord." And he subjoins immediately why we are still "absent or in pilgrimage," tho we have now believed; "For we walk by faith," he says; "not by sight."

V. Our whole business, then, brethren, in this life is to heal this eye of the heart whereby God may be seen. To this end are celebrated the Holy Mysteries; to this end is preached the Word of God; to this end are the moral exhortations of the Church, those, that is, that relate to the corrections of manners, to the amendment of carnal lusts, to the renouncing the world, not in word only, but in a change of life: to this end is directed the whole aim of the Divine and Holy Scriptures, that that inner man may be purged of that which hinders us from the sight of God. For as the eye which is formed to see this temporal light, a light tho heavenly yet corporeal, and manifest, not to men only, but even to the meanest animals (for this the eye is formed to this light); if anything be thrown or falls into it, whereby it is disordered, is shut out from this light; and tho it encompasses the eye with its presence, yet the eye turns itself away from, and is absent from it; and tho its disordered condition is not only rendered absent from the light which is present, but the light to see which it was formed is even painful to it, so the eye of the heart too, when it is disordered and wounded, turns away from the light of righteousness, and dares not and can not contemplate it.

VI. And what is it that disorders the eye of the heart? Evil desire, covetousness, injustice, worldly concupiscence; these disorder, close, blind the eye of the heart. And yet, when the eye of the body is out of order, how is the physician sought out, what an absence of all delay to open and cleanse it, that they may be healed whereby this outward light is seen! There is running to and fro, no one is still, no one loiters, if even the smallest straw fall into the eye. And God, it must be allowed, made the sun which we desire to see with sound eyes. Much brighter, assuredly, is He who made it; nor is the light with which the eye of the mind is concerned of this kind at all. That light is eternal wisdom. God made thee, O man, after His own image. Would He give thee wherewithal to see the sun which He made, and not give thee wherewithal to see Him who made thee, when He made thee after His own image? He hath given thee this also; both hath He given thee. But much thou dost love these outward eyes, and despisest much that interior eye; it thou dost carry about bruised and wounded. Yea, it would be a punishment to, if thy Maker should wish to manifest Himself unto thee, it would be a punishment to thine eye, before that it is cured and healed. For so Adam in Paradise sinned, and hid himself from the face of God. As long, then, as he had the sound heart of a pure conscience, he rejoiced at the presence of God; when that eye was wounded by sin, he began to dread the divine light, he fled back into the darkness, and the thick covert of trees, flying from the truth, and anxious for the shade.

VII. Therefore, my brethren, since we too are born of him, and as the apostle says, "In Adam all die"; for we were all at first two persons; if we were loath to obey the physician, that we might not be sick; let us obey Him now, that we may be delivered from sickness. The Physician gave us precepts, when we were whole; He gave us precepts that we might not need a physician. "They that are whole," He saith, "need not a physician, but they that are sick." When whole, we despised these precepts, and by experience have felt how to our own destruction we despised His precepts. Now we are sick, we are in distress, we are on the bed of weakness; yet let us not despair. For because we could not come to the Physician, He hath vouchsafed to come Himself to us. Tho despised by man when he was whole, He did not despise him when he was stricken. He did not leave off to give other precepts to the weak, who would not keep the first precepts, that he might not be weak; as tho He would say, "Assuredly thou hast by experience felt that I spoke the truth when I said, Touch not this. Be healed then now, at length, and recover the life thou hast lost. Lo, I am bearing thine infirmity; drink then the bitter cup. For thou hast of thine own self made those my so sweet precepts, which were given to thee when whole, so toilsome. They were despised, and so thy distress began; cured thou canst not be, except thou drink the bitter cup, the cup of temptations, wherein this life abounds, the cup of tribulation, anguish, and suffering. Drink then," He says, "drink, that thou mayest live." And that the sick man may not make answer, "I can not, I can not bear it, I will not drink"; the Physician, all whole tho He be, drinketh first, that the sick man may not hesitate to drink. For what bitterness is there in this cup which He hath not drunk? If it be contumely, He heard it first when He drove out the devils. "He hath a devil, and by Beelzebub He casteth out devils." Whereupon, in order to comfort the sick, He saith, "If they have called the Master of the house Beelzebub, how much more shall they call them of His household?" If pains are this bitter cup, He was bound, and scourged, and crucified. If death be this bitter cup, He died also. If infirmity shrink with horror from any particular kind of death, none was at that time more ignominious than the death of the cross. For it was not in vain that the apostle, when setting forth His obedience, added, "He became obedient unto death, even the death of the cross."

VIII. But because He designed to honor His faithful ones at the end of the world, He hath first honored the cross in this world;

in such wise that the princes of the earth who believe in Him have prohibited any criminal from being crucified; and that cross which the Jewish persecutors with great mockery prepared for the Lord, even kings, His servants, at this day, bear with great confidence on their foreheads. Only the shameful nature of the death which our Lord vouchsafed to undergo for us is not now so apparent, Who, as the apostle says, "Was made a curse for us." And when, as He hung, the blindness of the Jews mocked Him, surely He could have come down from the cross, who, if He had not so willed, had not been on the cross; but it was a greater thing to rise from the grave than to come down from the cross. Our Lord, then, in doing these divine and in suffering these human things, instructs us by His bodily miracles and bodily patience, that we may believe and be made whole to behold those things invisible which the eye of the body hath no knowledge of. With this intent, then, He cured those blind men of whom the account has just now been read in the Gospel. And consider what instruction He has by this cure conveyed to the man who is sick within.

IX. Consider the issue of the thing, and the order of the circumstances. Those two blind men sitting by the wayside cried out, as the Lord passed by, that He would have mercy upon them. But they were restrained

AUGUSTINE

from crying out by the multitude which was with the Lord. Now do not suppose that this circumstance is left without a mysterious meaning. But they overcame the crowd who kept them back by the great perseverance of their cry, that their voice might reach the Lord's ears; as tho he had not already anticipated their thoughts. So then the two blind men cried out that they might be heard by the Lord, and could not be restrained by the multitude. The Lord "was passing by," and they cried out. The Lord "stood still," and they were healed. "For the Lord Jesus stood still, and called them, and said, What wilt ye that I shall do unto you? They say unto Him, That our eyes may be opened." The Lord did according to their faith, He recovered their eyes. If we have now understood by the sick, the deaf, the dead, the sick, and deaf, and dead within; let us look out in this place also for the blind within. The eyes of the heart are closed; Jesus passeth by that we may cry out. What is meant by "Jesus passeth by?" Jesus is doing things which last but for a time. What is meant by "Jesus passeth by?" Jesus doth things which pass by. Mark and see how many things of His have passed by. He was born of the Virgin Mary; is He being born always? As an infant He was suckled; is He suckled always? He ran through the successive ages of life until man's full estate; doth He grow in body always?

Boyhood succeeded to infancy, to boyhood youth, to youth man's full stature in several passing successions. Even the very miracles which He did are passed by; they are read and believed. For because these miracles are written that so they might be read, they passed by when they were being done. In a word, not to dwell long on this, He was crucified; is He hanging on the cross always? He was buried, He rose again, He ascended into heaven, now He dieth no more, death hath no more dominion over Him. And His divinity abideth ever, yea, the immortality of His body now shall never fail. But nevertheless all those things which were wrought by Him in time have passed by; and they are written to be read, and they are preached to be believed. In all these things, then, Jesus passeth by.

X. And what are the two blind men by the wayside but the two people to cure whom Jesus came? Let us show these two people in the Holy Scriptures. It is written in the Gospel, "Other sheep I have which are not of this fold; them also must I bring, that there may be one fold and one Shepherd." Who then are the two people? One the people of the Jews, and the other of the Gentiles. "I am not sent," He saith, "but unto the lost sheep of the house of Israel." To whom did He say this? To the disciples; when that woman of Canaan, who confest herself to be a dog, cried out that she might be found worthy of the crumbs from the Master's table. And because she was found worthy, now were the two people to whom He had come made manifest, the Jewish people, to wit, of whom He said, "I am not sent but unto the lost sheep of the house of Israel"; and the people of the Gentiles, whose type this woman exhibited, whom He had first rejected, saying, "It is not meet to cast the children's bread to the dogs"; and to whom, when she said, "Truth, Lord, yet the dogs eat of the crumbs which fall from their master's table," He answered, "O woman, great is thy faith; be it unto thee even as thou wilt." For of this people also was that centurion of whom the same Lord saith, "Verily I say unto you, I have not found so great faith, no, not in Israel," because he had said, "I am not worthy that Thou shouldst come under my roof, but speak the word only, and my servant shall be healed." So then the Lord even before His passion and glorification pointed out two people, the one to whom He had come because of the promises to the Fathers, and the other whom for His mercy's sake He did not reject; that it might be fulfilled which had been promised to Abraham, "In thy seed shall all the nations be blessed."

XI. Attend, now, dearly beloved. The Lord was passing by, and the blind men cried out. What is this "passing by?" As we have already said, He was doing works which passed by. Now upon these passing works is our faith built up. For we believe on the Son of God, not only in that He is the Word of God, by whom all things were made; for if He had always continued in the form of God, equal with God, and had not emptied Himself in taking the form of a servant, the blind men would not even have perceived Him, that they might be able to cry out. But when he wrought passing works, that is, when He humbled Himself, having become obedient unto death, even the death of the cross, the two blind men cried out, Have mercy on us, thou Son of David. For this very thing that He, David's Lord and Creator, willed also to be David's son, He wrought in time, He wrought passing by.

XII. Now what is it, brethren, to cry out unto Christ, but to correspond to the grace of Christ by good works? This I say, brethren, lest haply we cry aloud with our voices, and in our lives be dumb. Who is he that crieth out to Christ, that his inward blindness may be driven away by Christ as He is passing by, that is, as He is dispensing to us those temporal sacraments, whereby we are instructed to receive the things which are eternal? Who is he that crieth out unto Christ? Whoso despiseth the world, crieth out unto Christ. Whoso despiseth the pleasures of the world, crieth out unto Christ. Whoso saith, not with his tongue but with his life, the world is crucified unto me, and I unto the world, crieth out unto Christ. Whoso disperseth abroad and giveth to the poor, that his righteousness may endure forever, crieth out unto Christ. For let him that hears, and is not deaf to the sound, sell that ye have, and give to the poor; provide yourselves bags which wax not old, a treasure in the heavens that faileth not; let him as he hears the sound as it were of Christ's footsteps passing by cry out in response to this in his blindness; that is, let him do these things. Let his voice be in his actions. Let him begin to despise the world, to distribute to the poor his goods, to esteem as nothing worth what other men love, let him disregard injuries, not seek to be avenged, let him give his cheek to the smiter, let him pray for his enemies; if any one who have taken away his goods, let him not ask for them again; if he have taken anything from any man, let him restore fourfold.

XIII. When he shall begin to do all this, all his kinsmen, relations, and friends will be in commotion. They who love the world will oppose him. What madness this! You are too extreme! What! Are not other men Christians? This is folly, this is madness. And other such like things do the multitude cry out to prevent the blind from crying out.

The multitude rebuked them as they cried out; but did not overcome their cries. Let them who wish to be healed understand what they have to do. Jesus is now also passing by; let them who are by the wayside cry out. These are they, who know God with their lips, but their heart is far from Him. These are by the wayside, to whom, as blinded in heart, Jesus gave His precepts. For when those passing things which Jesus did are recounted, Jesus is always represented to us as passing by. For even unto the end of the world there will not be wanting blind men sitting by the wayside. Need then there is that they who sit by the wayside should cry out. The multitude that was with the Lord would repress the crying of those who were seeking for recovery. Brethren, do you see my meaning? For I know not how to speak, but still less do I know how to be silent. I will speak then, and speak plainly. For I fear Jesus passing by and Jesus standing still; and therefore I can not keep silence. Evil and unknown Christians hinder good Christians who are truly earnest and wish to do the commandments of God, which are written in the Gospel. This multitude which is with the Lord hinders those who are crying out, hinders those, that is, who are doing well, that they may not by perseverance be healed. But let them cry out, and not faint; let them not be led away as if by the authority of numbers; let them not imitate those who become Christians before them, who live evil lives themselves, and are jealous of the good deeds of others. Let them not say, "Let us live as these so many live." Why not rather as the Gospel ordains? Why dost thou wish to live according to the remonstrances of the multitude who would hinder them, and not after the steps of the Lord who passeth by? They will mock, and abuse, and call thee back; do thou cry out till thou reach the ears of Jesus. For they who shall persevere in doing such things as Christ hath enjoined, and regard not the multitude that hinder them, nor think much of their appearing to follow Christ, that is of their being called Christians; but who love the light which Christ is about to restore to them more than they fear the uproar of those who are hindering them; they shall on no account be separated from Him, and Jesus will stand still, and make them whole.

XIV. For how are our eyes made whole? That as by faith we perceive Christ passing by in the temporal economy, so we may attain to the knowledge of Him as standing still in His unchangeable eternity. For there is the eye made whole when the knowledge of Christ's divinity is attained. Let your love apprehend this; attend ye to the great mystery which I am to speak of. All the things which were done by our Lord Jesus Christ, in time, graft faith in us. We believe on the

Son of God, not on the word only, by whom all things were made; but on this very word, "made flesh that He might dwell among us"; who was born of the Virgin Mary; and the rest which the Faith contains, and which are represented to us that Christ might pass by, and that the blind, hearing His footsteps as He passeth by, might by their works cry out, by their life exemplifying the profession of their faith. But now in order that they who cry out may be made whole, Jesus standeth still. For he saw Jesus now standing still, who says, "Though we have known Christ after the flesh, yet now henceforth know we Him no more." For he saw Christ's divinity as far as in this life is possible. There is then in Christ the divinity, and the humanity. The divinity standeth still, the humanity passeth by. What means "the divinity standeth still?" It changeth not, is not shaken, doth not depart away. For He did not so come to us as to depart from the Father; nor did He so ascend as to change His place. When He assumed flesh, it changed place; but God assuming flesh, seeing He is not in place, doth not change His place. Let us then be touched by Christ standing still, and so our eyes be made whole. But whose eyes? The eyes of those who cry out when He is passing by; that is, who do good works through that faith which hath been dispersed in time, to instruct in our infancy.

AUGUSTINE

XV. Now what thing more precious can we have than the eye made whole? They rejoice who see this created light which shines from heaven, or even that which is given out from a lamp. And how wretched do they seem who can not see this light? But wherefore do I speak, and talk of all these things, but to exhort you all to cry out, when Jesus passeth by. I hold up this light which perhaps ye do not see as an object of love to you, holy brethren. Believe, while as yet ye see it not; and cry out that ye may see. How great is thought to be the unhappiness of men who do not see this bodily light? Does any one become blind; immediately it is said: "God is angry with him, he has committed some wicked deed." So said Tobias's wife to her husband. He cried out because of the kid, lest it had come of theft; he did not like to hear the sound of any stolen thing in his house; and she, maintaining what she had done, reproached her husband; and when he said, "Restore it if it be stolen"; she answered insultingly, "Where are thy righteous deeds?" How great was her blindness who maintaineth the theft; and how clear a light he saw, who commanded the stolen thing to be restored! She rejoiced outwardly in the light of the sun; he inwardly in the light of righteousness. Which of them was in the better light?

XVI. It is to the love of this light that I

would exhort you, beloved; that ye would cry out by your works, when the Lord passeth by; let the voice of faith sound out, that Jesus was standing still, that is, the unchangeable, abiding wisdom of God, and the majesty of the Word of God, by which all things were made, may open your eyes. The same Tobias, in giving advice to his son, instructed him to this, to cry out; that is, he instructed him to good works. He told him to give to the poor, charged him to give alms to the needy, and taught him, saying, "My son, alms suffereth not to come into darkness." The blind gave counsel for receiving and gaining sight. "Alms," saith he, "suffereth not to come into darkness." Had his son in astonishment answered him, "What then, father, hast thou not given alms, that thou speakest to me in blindness; art not thou in darkness, and yet thou dost say to me, Alms suffereth not to come into darkness?" But no, he knew well what the light was concerning which he gave his son instruction, he knew well what he saw in the inner man. The son held out his hand to his father, to enable him to dwell in heaven.

XVII. To be brief; that I may conclude this sermon, brethren, with a matter which touches me very nearly, and gives me much pain, see what crowds there are which rebuke the blind as they cry out. But let them not deter you. whosoever among this crowd desire to be healed; for there are many Christians in name, and in works ungodly; let them not deter you from good works. Cry out amid the crowds that are restraining you, and calling you back, and insulting you, whose lives are evil. For not only by their voices, but by evil works, do wicked Christians repress the good. A good Christian has no wish to attend the public shows. In this very thing, that he bridles his desire of going to the theater, he cries out after Christ, cries out to be healed. Others run together thither, but perhaps they are heathens or Jews? Ah! indeed, if Christians went not to the theaters, there would be so few people there that they would go away for very shame. So then Christians run thither also, bearing the Holy Name only to their condemnation. Cry out then by abstaining from going, by repressing in thy heart this worldly concupiscence; hold on with a strong and persevering cry unto the ears of the Savior, that Jesus may stand still and heal thee. Cry out amid the very crowds, despair not of reaching the ears of the Lord. For the blind man in the Gospel did not cry out in that quarter where no crowd was, that so they might be heard in that direction, where there was no impediment from persons hindering them. Amid the very crowds they cried out; and yet the Lord heard them. And so also do ye even amid sinners, and sensual men, amid the lovers of the vanities of the world, there cry out that the Lord may heal you. Go not to another quarter to cry out unto the Lord, go not to heretics and cry out unto Him there. Consider, brethren, how in that crowd which was hindering them from crying out, even there they who cried out were made whole.

WYCLIF

CHRIST'S REAL BODY NOT IN THE EUCHARIST

BIOGRAPHICAL NOTE

JOHN WYCLIF, eminent as scholar, preacher, and translator, was born in 1324 in Spresswel, near Richmond, Yorkshire, England. Known as the "Morning Star of the Reformation" he was a vigorous and argumentative speaker, exemplifying his own definition of preaching as something which should be "apt, apparent, full of true feeling, fearless in rebuking sins, and so addrest to the heart as to enlighten the spirit and subdue the will." On these lines he organized a band of Bible preachers who worked largely among the common people.

Much of Wyclif's popularity was due to his clear and simple style. While not a great orator, he introduced a popular method of preaching that was widely copied. He died at Lutterworth in 1384. The Church considered him a heretic, for he taught the right of the individual to form his own opinions after personal study of the Scriptures. He was the first Englishman to translate the Bible systematically into his native Anglo-Saxon. In 1428, by order of Pope Martin V, his bones were exhumed and burned, and the ashes thrown into the river Swale.

WYCLIF
1324—1384

CHRIST'S REAL BODY NOT IN THE EUCHARIST

This is my body.—Matt. xxvi., 26.

NOW UNDERSTAND ye the words of our Savior Christ, as He spake them one after another—as Christ spake them. For He took bread and blest, and yet what blest He? The Scripture saith not that Christ took the bread and blest it, or that He blest the bread which He had taken. Therefore it seemeth more that He blest His disciples and apostles, whom He had ordained witnesses of His passion; and in them He left His blest word, which is the bread of life, as it is written, "Not only in bread liveth man, but in every word that proceedeth out of the mouth of God." Also Christ saith, "I am the bread of life that came down from heaven." And Christ saith also in John, "The words that I have spoken to you are spirit and life." Therefore it seemeth more that He blest His disciples, and also His apostles, in whom the bread of life was left more than in material bread, for the material bread hath an end. As it is written in the Gospel of Matthew xv.

that Christ said, "All things that a man eateth go down into the belly, and are sent down into the draught;" but the blessing of Christ kept His disciples and apostles, both bodily and [ghostly] spiritual. As it is written, that none of them perished but the son of perdition, that the Scriptures might be fulfilled, and often the Scripture saith that Jesus took bread and brake it, and gave it to his disciples, and said, "Take ye, eat ye, this is my body that shall be given for you." But He said not this bread is my body, or that bread should be given for the life of the world. For Christ saith, What and if ye shall see the Son of man ascend up where He was before? "It is the Spirit that quickeneth, the flesh profiteth nothing." Also Christ saith in the Gospel, "Verily, verily I say unto you except the wheat corn fall into the ground and die, it abideth alone, but if it die it bringeth forth much fruit."

Here men may see by the words of Christ that it behooved that He died in the flesh, and that in His death was made the fruit of everlasting life for all them that believe on Him, as it is written "For as by Adam they all die, even so by Christ shall all live, and every man in his own order; for as one clearness is in the sun, another in the moon, and a star in clearness is nothing in comparison to the sun; even so is the rising again of the dead for we are sown in corruption and shall rise again incorruptible, we are sown in infirmity, and shall rise again in strength; we are sown in natural bodies, and shall rise again spiritual bodies." Then if Christ shall change thus our deadly bodies by death, and God the Father spared not his own Son, as it is written, but that death should reign in him as in us, and that he should be translated into a spiritual body, as the first rising again of dead men; then how say the hypocrites that take on them to make our Lord's body? Make they the glorified body? Either make they again the spiritual body which is risen from death to life or make they the fleshy body as it was before he suffered death? And if they say also that they make the spiritual body of Christ, it may not be so, for what Christ said and did, He did as He was at supper before He suffered His passion; as it is written that the spiritual body of Christ rose again from death to life. Also that He ascended up to heaven, and that He will abide there till He come to judge the quick and the dead. And if they say that they make Christ's body as it was before He had suffered His passion, then must they needs grant that Christ is to die yet. For by all Holy Scriptures He was promised to die, and that He should give lordship of everlasting life.

Furthermore, if they say that Christ made His body of bread, I ask, With what words made He it? Not with these words, *Hoc est corpus meum;* that is to say in English, "This is my body," for they are the words of giving, and not of making, which He said after that He brake the bread; then parting it among His disciples and apostles. Therefore if Christ had made of that bread His body, [He] had made it in His blessing, or else in giving of thanks, and not in the words of giving; for if Christ had spoken of the material bread that He had in His hands when He said, *Hoc est corpus meum,* "This is my body," it was made before, or else the word had been a lie. For if I say, This is my hand, and if it be not a hand, then am I a liar; therefore seek carefully if ye can find two words of blessing, or of giving of thanks, wherewith Christ made his body and blood of the bread and wine. And that all the clerks of the earth know not, for if ye might find or know those words, then should ye wax great masters above Christ, and then ye might be givers of His substance, and as fathers and makers of Him, and that He should worship you, as it is written, Thou shalt worship thy father and mother. Of such as desire such worship against God's law, speaketh St. Paul of the man of sin, that enhanceth himself as if he were God. And he is worshiped over all things as God, and showeth himself as he were God. Where our clergy are guilty in this, judge ye or they that know most, for they say that when ye have said, *Hoc est corpus meum,* that is to say,

"This is my body;" which ye call the words of consecration, or else of making; and when they are said over the bread, ye say that there is left no bread, but it is the body of the Lord. So that in the bread there remaineth nothing but a heap of accidents, as witness ruggedness, roundness, savor, touching, and tasting, and such other accidents. Then, if thou sayest that the flesh and blood of Christ, that is to say, his manhood, is made more, or increased by so much as the ministration of bread and wine is, the which ye minister—if ye say it is so—then thou must needs consent that the thing which is not God to-day shall be God to-morrow; yea, and that the thing which is without spirit of life, but groweth in the field by kind, shall be God at another time. And we all ought to believe that He was without beginning, and without ending; and not made, for if the manhood of Christ were increased every day by so much as the bread and wine draweth to that ye minister, He should increase more in one day by cart-loads than He did in thirty-two years when He was here in earth.

And if thou makest the body of the Lord in those words, *Hoc est corpus meum;* that is to say, "This is my body"; and if thou mayest make the body of the Lord in those words, "This is my body," thou thyself must be the person of Christ, or else there is a false God; for if it be thy body as thou sayest, then it is the body of a false knave or of a drunken man, or of a thief, or of a lecherer, or full of other sins, and then there is an unclean body for any man to worship for God! For even if Christ had made there His body of material bread in the said words, as I know they are not the words of making, what earthly man had power to do as He did? For in all Holy Scripture, from the beginning of Genesis to the end of the Apocalypse, there are no words written of the making of Christ's body; but there are written that Christ was the Son of the Father, and that He was conceived of the Holy Ghost, and that He took flesh and blood of the Virgin Mary, and that He was dead, and that He rose again from death on the third day, and that He ascended to heaven very God and man, and that we should believe in all Scriptures that are written of Him, and that He is to come to judge the quick and the dead, and that the same Christ Jesus, King and Savior, was at the beginning with the Father and the Holy Ghost, making all things of naught, both heaven and earth, and all things that are therein; working by word of His virtue, for He said, Be it done, and it was done, whose works never earthly man might comprehend, either make. And yet the words of the making of these things are written in the beginning of Genesis, even as God spake them; and if ye can not make the work that He made, and have the word by which He made it, how shall ye make Him that made the works? You have no words of authority or power left you on earth by which ye should do this, but ye have feigned this craft of your false errors, which some of you understand not; for it is prophesied, "They shall have eyes and see not, and ears and hear not; and shall see prophesies, and shall not understand, less they be converted; for I hide them from the hearts of those people; their hearts are greatly fatted." And this thing is done to you for the wickedness of your errors in unbelief; therefore be ye converted from the worst sin, as it is written, "When Moses was in the hill with God," the people made a calf and worshiped it as God. And God spake to Moses, "Go, for the people have done the worst sin to make and worship alien gods."

But now I shall ask you a word; answer ye me, Whether is the body of the Lord made at once or at twice? Is it both the flesh and the blood in the host of the bread; or else is the flesh made at one time, and the blood made at another time; that is to say, the wine in the chalice? If thou wilt say it is full and wholly the manhood of Christ in the host of bread, both flesh and blood, skin, hair, and bones, then makest thou us to worship a false god in the chalice, which is unconjured when ye worship the bread; and if ye say the flesh is in the bread, and the blood in the wine, then thou must grant, if thy craft be true, as it is not indeed, that the manhood of Christ is parted, and that He is made at two times. For first thou takest the host of bread, or a piece of bread, and makest it as ye say, and the innocent people worship it. And then thou takest to thee the chalice, and likewise marrest, makest, I would have said, the blood in it, and then they worship it also, and if it be so as I am sure that the flesh and blood of Christ ascended, then are ye false harlots to God and to us; for when we shall be houselled ye bring to us the dry flesh, and let the blood be away; for ye give us after the bread, wine and water, and sometimes clean water unblest, or rather conjured, by the virtue of your craft; and yet ye say, under the host of bread is the full manhood of Christ. Then by your own confession must it needs be that we worship a false god in the chalice, which is unconjured when we worship the bread, and worship the one as the other; but where find ye that ever Christ or any of His disciples taught any man to worship this bread or wine?

Therefore, what shall we say of the apostles that were so much with Christ, and were called by the Holy Ghost; had they forgotten to set it in the creed when they made it, which is Christian men's belief? Or else we might say that they knew no such God, for they believe in no more gods but in Him that was at the beginning, and made of naught all things visible and invisible, which Lord took flesh and blood, being in the Virgin, the same God. But ye have many false ways, to beguile the innocent people with sleights of the fiend.

For ye say that in every host each piece is the whole manhood of Christ, or full substance of Him. For ye say as a man may take a glass, and break the glass into many pieces, and in every piece properly thou mayest see thy face, and yet thy face is not parted; so ye say the Lord's body is in each host or piece, and His body is not parted. And this is a full subtle question to beguile an innocent fool, but will ye take heed of this subtle question, how a man may take a glass and behold the very likeness of his own face, and yet it is not his face, but the likeness of his face; for if it were his very face, then he must needs have two faces, one on his body and another in the glass. And if the glass were broken in many places, so there should be many faces more by the glass than by the body, and each man shall make as many faces to them as they would; but as ye may see the mind or likeness of your face, which is not the very face; but the figure thereof, so the bread is the figure or mind of Christ's body in earth, and therefore Christ said, As oft as ye do this thing do it in mind of me.

Also ye say this, As a man may light many

candles at one candle, and yet the light of that candle is never the more nor ever the less; so ye say that the manhood of Christ descendeth into each part of every host, and the manhood of Christ is never the more nor less. Where then becometh your ministrations? For if a man light many candles at one candle, as long as they burn there will be many candles lighted, and as well the last candle as the first; and so by this reason, if ye shall fetch your word at God, and make God, there must needs be many gods, and that is forbidden in the first commandment, Exod. xx. And as for making more, either making less, of Christ's manhood, it lieth not in your power to come there nigh, neither to touch it, for it is ascended into heaven in a spiritual body, which He suffered not Mary Magdalen to touch, when her sins were forgiven to her.

Therefore all the sacraments that are left here in earth are but minds of the body of Christ, for a sacrament is no more to say but a sign or mind of a thing passed, or a thing to come; for when Jesus spake of the bread, and said to His disciples, As ye do this thing, do it in mind of me, it was set for a mind of good things passed of Christ's body; but when the angel showed to John the sacraments of the woman and of the beast that bare her, it was set for a mind of evil things to come on the face of the earth, and great destroying of the people of God. And in the old law there were many figures or minds of things to come. For before Christ, circumcision was commanded by a law; and he that kept not the law was slain. And yet St. Paul saith, "And neither is it circumcision that is openly in the flesh, but he that is circumcised of heart in spirit, not the letter whose praising is not of men, but of God." Peter saith in the third chapter of his epistle, "And so baptism of like form maketh not us safe, but the putting away of the filthiness of the flesh, and the having of good conscience in God by the rising again of our Lord Jesus Christ from death, that we should be made heirs of everlasting life, He went up into heaven, and angels, and powers, and virtues, are made subjects to Him.

And also the Scripture saith of John Baptist, that he preached in the wilderness and said, "A stronger than I shall come after me, and I am not worthy to kneel down and unlace His shoe;" and yet Christ said that he was more than a prophet. See also Isaiah xl., Matt. xi. How may ye then say that ye are worthy to make His body, and yet your works bear witness that ye are less than the prophets? for if ye were not, ye should not teach the people to worship the sacraments or minds of Christ for Christ himself; which sacraments or figures are lawful as God taught them and left them unto us, as the sacrifices or minds of the old law were full good. As it is written, "They that kept them should live in them." And so the bread that Christ brake was left to us for mind of things passed for the body of Christ, that we should believe He was a very man in kind as we are, but as God in power, and that His manhood was sustained by food as ours. For St. Paul saith He was very man, and in form he was found as man. And so we must believe that He was very God and very man together, and that He ascended up very God and very man to heaven, and that He shall be there till He come to doom the world. And we may not see him bodily, being in this life, as it is written, Peter i., for he saith, "Whom ye have not seen ye love, into whom ye now not seeing believe." And John saith in the first chapter of his Gospel, "No man saw God; none but the only begotten Son that is in the bosom of the Father, He hath told it out." And John saith in his first epistle, the third chapter, "Every man that sinneth seeth not him, neither knoweth him." By what reason then say ye that are sinners that ye make God? truly this must needs be the worst sin, to say that ye make God, and it is the abomination of discomfort that is said in Daniel the prophet to be standing in the holy place; he that readeth let him understand.

Also Luke saith that Christ took the cup after that He had supped, and gave thanks and said, "This cup is the new testament in my blood that shall be shed unto the remission of sins for man." Now, what say ye; the cup which He said was the new testament in His blood, was it a material cup in which the wine was that He gave his disciples wine of, or was it His most blest body in which the blest blood was kept till it was shed out for the sins of them that should be made safe by His passion? Needs must we say that He spake of His holy body, as He did when He called His passion or suffering in body a cup, when He prayed to His father, before He went to His passion, and said, "If it be possible that this cup pass from me, but if thou wilt that I drink it, thy will be done?" He spake not here of the material cup in which He had given His disciples drink; for it troubled not Him, but He prayed for His great sufferance and bitter death, the which He suffered for our sins and not for His own. And if He spake of His holy body and passion when He said, "This cup is the new testament in my blood," so He spake of His holy body when He said, "This is my body which shall be given for you," and not of the material bread which He had in His hand. Also in another place He called His passion a cup, where the mother of Zebedee's sons came to Him, and asked of Him that her two sons, when He came to His kingdom, might sit one on His right, and one at His left side. And He answered and said, "Woman, thou wottest not what thou asketh; then He said to them, May ye drink of the cup that I shall drink? and they said, Yea, Lord. And He said, Ye shall drink of my cup, but to sit on my right hand or left hand it is not mine to give, but to the Father it is proper." But in that He said, Ye shall drink of my cup, He promised them to suffer tribulation of this world as He did, by the which they should enter into life everlasting, and to be both on his right hand. And thus ye may see that Christ spake not of the material cup, neither of himself, nor of his apostles, neither of material bread, neither of material wine. Therefore let every man wisely, with meek prayers, and great study, and also charity, read the words of God and holy Scriptures; but many of you are like the mother of Zebedee's sons to whom Christ said, "Thou knowest not what thou askest." So, many of you know not what ye ask, nor what you do; for if ye did, ye would not blaspheme God as ye do, to set an alien God instead of the living God. Also Christ saith, "I am a very vine; wherefore then worship ye not the vine God, as ye do the bread? Wherein was Christ a very vine, or wherein was the bread Christ's body, in figurative speech, which is hidden to the understanding? Then if Christ became not a material or an earthly vine, neither did a material vine become His body. So neither the bread, material bread, was changed from its substance to the flesh and blood of Christ.

Have ye not read in John the second, when Christ came into the temple, they asked of Him what token He would show, that they might believe Him. And He answered them, "Cast down this temple, and in three days I shall raise it again;" which words were fulfilled in His rising again from death; but when He said, "Undo this temple," in that that He said this, they were in error, for they understood it fleshly, and had supposed that He had spoken of the temple of Jerusalem, because He stood in it. And therefore they accused Him at His passion full falsely. For He spake of the temple of His blest body, which rose again in the third day. And right so Christ spake of His holy body when He said, "This is my body which shall be given for you," which was given to death, and to rising again to bliss, for all that shall be saved by him. But like as they accused him falsely of the temple of Jerusalem, so now a days they accuse falsely against Christ, and say that Christ spake of the bread that He brake among His apostles; for in that Christ said this, they are deceived, take it fleshly, and turn it to the material bread, as the Jews did to the temple; and on this false understanding they make abomination of discomfort, as is said by Daniel the prophet, and in Matthew xxiv., to be standing in the holy place; he that readeth let him understand.

Now, therefore, pray we heartily to God,

that this evil may be made short for the chosen men, as He hath promised in His blest Gospel; and the large and broad way that leadeth to perdition may be stopt, and the straight and narrow way that leadeth to bliss may be made open by Holy Scriptures, that we may know which is the will of God, to serve Him in truth and holiness in the dread of God, that we may find by Him a way of bliss everlasting. So be it.

SAVONAROLA

THE ASCENSION OF CHRIST

BIOGRAPHICAL NOTE

Girolamo Savonarola was born at Ferrara in 1452, and was admitted in 1475 into the novitiate of the Dominican Order, where he soon made himself conspicuous for eloquence, and in Florence attracted many hearers by his diatribes against corruption. Florence, having lost its independence as a republic, was completely under the sway of the Medici, who became arrayed against Savonarola, who aimed at establishing an ideal Christian commonwealth. When he attacked the Pope Alexander VI. his doom was practically sealed. In 1495 he was forbidden to appear in the pulpit, and four years later was excommunicated. He rebelled against papal authority, but the people of Florence grew tired of the strict rule of conduct imposed by his teaching, and he was imprisoned and tried for heresy and sedition. On May 23, 1498, he was hanged and his body burned. His puritanism, his bold rebuking of vice, his defiance of every authority excepting that of his own conscience, seem to anticipate the efforts made by Calvin to regenerate Geneva. Both men failed in their splendid attempts at social reformation, but both left an example of heroic altho somewhat short-sighted unselfishness, which has borne fruit in history.

SAVONAROLA

1452—1498

THE ASCENSION OF CHRIST [1]

While he blessed them, he was parted from them, and carried up into heaven.—Luke xxiv., 51.

BELOVED in Christ Jesus, the wise men of this world divide all created things into two classes; one class they name substances, the other accidents. The substances are those things that exist through themselves without requiring anything else on which to rest, as the earth, water, air, the heavens, animals, stones, plants, and similar things. The accidents can not exist by themselves, but only by resting on something else, as color, odor, taste, and other such things. But because our knowledge is entirely through the senses, and we are able to know anything only when its accidents fall upon our senses, we have, therefore, knowledge of the accidents rather than of the substances. The eyes are for colors, the ears for sounds, the nose for scents, the tongue for flavors, the touch for heat and cold, for hard and soft. Each sense has its own sphere of knowledge and brings what it

[1] Reprinted by permission of Messrs. G. P. Putnam's Sons from "The World's Orations," the translation having been copyrighted by Messrs. Putnams.

has perceived before the imagination, and this hands it over to the reason within, which reads and illuminates the productions of the imagination, judges them, and in this way comes to a knowledge of the substances. But the reason has little light if it is separated from the body, for God has joined soul and body together; and so by means of the senses knowledge becomes definite and complete. For if the soul out of the body were richer in knowledge, it would be in vain that it should be in the body. God and nature have done nothing in vain, and therefore the soul's union with the body ministers to its perfection.

The soul's knowledge, however, will not be complete so long as it lives in this mortal body. It does not while here come to the fundamental distinctions and causes of the substances, because it is obliged to know the inner side of things through their externals. Therefore man is able only imperfectly to know an incorporeal substance; how much less can he know the uncreated infinite being of God? But if he can not know the being of God, he will not be able to know many other infinite things which are in Him. We ought therefore not to be surprised that there is much in God which we can not understand, and that very many truths of the faith we can not yet prove since we do not yet know everything. The great God in His rich mercy saw our poor knowledge and came into our flesh and assumed it that He might work for us, die, and rise again from the dead; until after a life full of love He raised Himself above the world of sense into His eternity. But so long as our Redeemer lived with His apostles they loved too much that which they saw of Him, because they were bound down to their senses, and were therefore unable to rise to the knowledge of His Spirit. It was necessary that He should disappear in the heavens that He might lift their souls far above the world of sense up to Himself. Their natural powers could not do this; therefore He gave to His elect a light from above. Ascending on high He led captivity captive, for ascending into the heavens He took with Him the prey which the devil had made of the soul of men ever since the fall of our parents. The Lord has given gifts unto men (Eph. iv. 8), inasmuch as He has imparted to them the seven gifts of the Holy Ghost. Now they leave everything of this world, and rise above by following Christ, who gives to them for a light the light of faith. Let us speak this morning of this faith which leads to the Savior.

"Awake thou that sleepest and Christ shall give thee light." Be not held captive by flesh and sense, which hold thee fast in sleep; rise to Christ, He will give thee light. See, His flesh is above. What do ye say to that, ye wise men of this world? Everything that has weight tends downward, but His flesh is on high above all heavens. This time your laws have been set at nought. But see what hope Almighty God rouses in us: if our head has gone above, we, His members, will follow Him. In that we hope; of that we preach; on that we live. Know, O man, that if thou wilt thou canst go to Paradise, for thither has thy Savior Christ gone; but know this also, that not by thine own nature, not by means of silver and gold, not by thy virtue, wilt thou reach that place. He has given gifts unto men, and through these thou mayest reach Paradise, if thou only wilt. He has given thee the gifts of His Holy Ghost, and before all the gift of knowledge by which He enlightens thee and shows thee by that light thy goal. Thereupon He gives thee the gift of wisdom, by which thou learnest to love thy goal, and perceivest how much thou needest love. Christ then says to man: Remain in My love, leave the things of this world, follow Me to heaven. And because it is needful for thee to know that this world amounts to nothing, He gives thee experience that it may say to thee that thou must soon leave this world in which nothing lasts. Through many difficulties and doubts, man must get so far and know what to do; therefore thou hast the gift of counsel. Hold fast to this counsel, and follow Christ, who will always give thee good counsel. He will give thee not the treasures of this world, but eternal glory and undying happiness. What wilt thou do, O child of man? Leave this world, enter the service of Christ. He is waiting for thee, and will reward thy service, for He is a bountiful rewarder. Let every one then hasten to serve Him. But because each one is bound to care for the salvation of his brother, and to lead him to Christ, therefore the Lord gives thee the gift of love, by which thou shouldst warn thy brother, thy neighbor, thy friend, thy wife, every one, and with all thy strength and zeal shouldst lead them to Christ. But in this world man must go through joy and sorrow. To oppose the joys of earth, Christ gives thee fear, that thou mightest always be careful lest thou shouldst fall, and not let thy joyous days separate thee from the grace of Christ: to oppose unhappiness, He gives thee strength to resist.

What do ye want, O children of men; will ye not follow Christ who has gone up on high and has departed to prepare a place for you in glory? Thou comest not into the service of the Lord, because thou art not able to believe these words. If thou didst but believe thou wouldst stand no longer indifferent. Thou art unbelieving, thou art unthankful, and the Lord will punish thy unbelief even as on the morning of His ascension He punished the unbelief of His apostles. Because I have explained to thee this morning this Gospel, I must punish the hardness and unthankfulness of thy heart. Thou hast refused the service of the Lord, who has ascended to prepare for thee the highest glory.

I call upon all men and women, all whose lives are ruined in sorrows and troubles. What do ye fear? He who believes that Christ is above no longer fears anything. Come then all ye into His service. Jesus reproved the unbelief and the hard-heartedness of His disciples, because they did not believe those who had seen Him after He had risen. Without faith it is impossible to please God. No doubt the apostles said: How can we believe these women? But these women were of pure heart before God, and therefore the Savior reproved His disciples. Ye deserve still sharper reprimands. To the disciples a few women announced the news that He had risen. Ye hear all this, and in addition all the glorious revelations in which the Lord after this manifested Himself on earth. Why do ye not come to serve Christ? Ye do not truly believe, because ye are so full of sin, and despise God's commandments. Ye do not deserve the gift of faith. He who has faith should show it in his deeds, that he may have what he says he has, and may know what he has; namely, the certainty of the divine word, which can not err, the goodness of God, and His guidance into all goodness. On account of thy sins, thou hast not the true light which would have enabled thee to see all goodness. Thou art sunk in vice, drunken with greed and luxury, and all the works of this world. Thou seekest only power and glory. And wherefore? If thou hadst faith, thou wouldst not seek such things, for thou wouldst know that faith would give thee a much higher crown. From these sins have come thy unbelief and thy hardness of heart. Therefore the words of faith do not touch thy heart: it is a heart of stone and iron. Throw off thy load of sin and give thy will to righteousness; then will thy hard-heartedness end, and God will bestow on thee the gift of faith. What wilt thou? Why standest thou so uncertain and irresolute? Why dost thou not hasten to Him, and see how He leaves thy life, how He goes into the heavens, to which He bids thee come up. Leave at length thy sensual life and enter the pathway of Christ. Hesitate no longer, begin to-day, put it not off until to-morrow. If thou hast faith, thou canst not delay longer, and if thy heart is right before God, He will give thee the light of faith which will enable thee to distinguish the false from the true faith, and so when on the right road not to fall into error. Then wilt thou know for thyself that the Gospel makes good men out of those who truly believe, and thine experience will tell thee that thou hast no occasion to doubt.

A story from the Old Testament might perhaps serve as a parable and make clearer what

I mean. When Balak heard of Israel's march, he was afraid and sent to call Balaam to curse Israel for him. Balaam set out on his way with his ass, accompanied by an angel of the Lord, because Balaam was going to Balak with an evil intention. The beast sought in vain to turn into the field, and finally fell down between two walls, and suffered under blows and curses, until the prophet saw the angel and perceived his sin. Balak is the devil who would ruin the people of God; by Balaam we can understand the nobles, the prelates, the preachers, the learned, who are held captive by their arrogance. The two servants are those who follow the proud, serve them, and flatter them, especially the lazy clergy and monks, who so far as outward show goes live a virtuous life, but who live for ceremonies and take care not to speak the truth. To these belong many citizens who live apparently virtuously and hide their pride. Because they commit no sins of the flesh which can be noticed, they are full of piety in their outward ceremonies, but within full of arrogance. These are the members of the devil, for the devil neither eats, drinks, nor sleeps, he is neither a miser nor a wanton, but is within full of pride as are these. By the ass we are to understand the simple people. They are led in the way of sin by the ceremonies of the lazy, since they are not thought fit for the worship of the heart, and must be led by masses, penance, and indulgences, and they throw away what might be of profit for money and for candles. The lazy give them council in their sermons: Give some vestment, build a chapel, and thou wilt be freed from any danger of going to hell. Do not believe these mountebanks; no outward act can bring you to Paradise, not even miracles and prophecy, but only the grace of God, if you have humility and love . . . . Before the ass stood an angel with a sword. This is Christ, who speaks to the ass: Walk no longer in the path of sin, for I have ready for you a great scourge. The ass alone saw the angel; for the simple first hear the word of the Lord, but Balaam and such as are with him will hear nothing of it. The ass left the path of captivity and went out into the field, into the way of the Lord. "For the kingdom of heaven is like treasure hid in a field; which when a man found he sold all that he had and bought that field." So the simple go into the holy field of the Scriptures and say: "Let me look around a little, for the flowers of this field bear fruit." Yea, our fathers, the prophets, apostles, and martyrs bore fruit, they who died with joy for the truth. These are they who go into the field and speak the truth in the face of death. Come into the city, where the nobles and the masters taken captive by sin crowd together, cry the lazy troop of monks: O fathers, it would be well if when you spoke of these things, you touched not this string, by which you allow yourselves to fall into disgrace and disfavor. They have said that already to me. Our persecution begins if we begin to preach. But Jesus was willing to die for the truth of what He said; should we forsake the truth in order not to displease men? No, we will say it in every way, and with Balaam's ass go into the field.

Think not that I am such a fool as to undertake these things without good reason. I call heaven and earth to witness against me if I do not speak the truth. For against all the world is my sermon; every one contradicts it. If I go about with lies, then I have Christ against me; therefore I have heaven and earth against me, and how then could I stand? As such a trifler with holy things how should I dare rise up? Believe me, I speak the truth, I have seen it with my eyes, and touched it with my hands. Believe it! If I speak not the truth, I consign myself body and soul to destruction; but I tell you I am certain of the truth, and I would that all were as I am. I say that of the truth on which I stand, not as tho I wished that others had my failings as well. So come then into the service of Jesus; come to the truth, come here, I bid you. Do ye not know how I explained the revelation of St. John? There were many who said that I spoke too much in detail, and went too deep into it. There stood the angel before the ass, and wanted it to go out into the field, but Balaam smote it; and ye know not how much opposition I must yet undergo. The lazy monks were the first who called me a fool and revolutionist, and on the other side stood the weak and the simple, who said in their innocent faith: "Oh, if we could only do what He teaches!" Then I had war with the citizens and the great judges of this time, whom my manner of preaching did not please. I was between two walls; the angel warned me, threatening eternal death from this road, and I received Balaam's blows. Ye know my persecution and my danger; but I knew that I was on the way to victory and said always: No human being can drive my cause from the world. Balaam, thou leanest thy foot against the walls, but do as thou wilt, I will crush thy foot; I leaned on the wall, on Christ, I leaned on His grace, I hoped; leave off thine anger and threatening, thou canst not get me away from the wall. I say to all of you: Come to the truth, forsake your vice and your malice, that I may not have to tell you of your grief. I say it to you, O Italy, I say it to you, O Rome, I say it to all of you; return and do penance. There stands before you the holy truth; she can not fall; she can not bend or give way; wait not until the blows fall.

In everything am I opprest; even the spiritual power is against me with Peter's mighty key. Narrow is my path and full of trouble; like Balaam's ass, I must throw myself on the ground and cry: "See, here I am; I am ready to die for the truth." But when Balaam beat his fallen beast, it said to him: "What have I done to thee?" So I say to you: "Come here and tell me: what have I done to you? Why do you beat me? I have spoken the truth to you; I have warned you to choose a virtuous life; I have led many souls to Christ." But you answer: "Thou hast spoken evil of us, therefore, thou shouldst suffer the stripes thou deservest." But I named no one, I only blamed your vices in general. If you have sinned, be angry with yourselves, not with me. I name none of you, but if the sins I have mentioned are without question yours, then they and not I make you known. As the smitten beast asked Balaam, so I ask you: "Tell me, am I not your ass? and do you not know that I have been obedient to you up to this very moment, that I have even done what my superiors have commanded, and have always behaved myself peaceably?" You know this, and because I am now so entirely different, you may well believe that a great cause drives me to it. Many knew me as I was at first; if I remained so I could have had as much honor as I wanted. I lived six years among you, and now I speak otherwise, nevertheless I announce to you the truth that is well known. You see in what sorrows and what opposition I must now live, and I can say with Jeremiah: "O, my mother, that thou hast borne me a man of strife and contention to the whole earth!" But where is a father or a mother that can say I have led their son into sin; one that can say I have ruined her husband or his wife? Everybody knows my manner of life, therefore it is right for you to believe that I speak the truth which everybody knows. You think that it is impossible for a man to do what the faith I have preached tells him to do: with God it would be easy for you.

The ass alone saw the angel, the others did not; so open your eyes. Thank God, many have them open. You have seen many learned men whom you thought wise, and they have withstood our cause: now they believe; many noted masters who were hard and proud against us: now humility casts them down. You have also seen many women turn from their vanity to simplicity; vicious youths who are now improved and conduct themselves in a new way. Many, indeed, have received this doctrine with humility. That doctrine has stood firm, no matter how attacked with the intention of showing that it was a doctrine opposed to Christ. God does that to manifest His wisdom, to show how it finally overcomes all other wisdom. And He is willing that His servants be spoken against that they may show their patience and humility, and for the sake of His love not be afraid of martyrdom.

O ye men and women, I bid you to this truth; let those who are in captivity contradict you as much as they will, God will come and oppose their pride. Ye proud, however, if you do not turn about and become better, then will the sword and the pestilence fall upon you; with famine and war will Italy be turned upside down. I foretell you this because I am sure of it: if I were not, I would not mention it. Open your eyes as Balaam opened his eyes when the angel said to him: "Had it not been for thine ass, I would have slain thee." So I say to you, ye captives: Had it not been for the good and their preaching, it would have been wo unto you. Balaam said: "If this way is not good, I will return." You say likewise, you would turn back to God, if your way is not good. And to the angel you say as Balaam said: "What wilt thou that we should do?" The angel answers thee as he answered Balaam: "Thou shalt not curse this people, but shalt say what I put in thy mouth." But in thy mouth he puts the warning that thou shouldst do good, convince one another of the divine truth, and bear evil manfully. For it is the life of a Christian to do good and to bear

SAVONAROLA

wrong and to continue stedfast unto death, and this is the Gospel, which we, according to the text of the Gospel for to-day, shall preach in all the world.

What wilt thou have of us, brother? you ask. I desire that you serve Christ with zeal and not with sloth and indifference. I desire that you do not mourn, but in thankfulness raise your hands to heaven, whenever your brother or your son enters the service of Christ. The time is come when Christ will work not only in you but through you and in others; whoever hears, let him say: "Come brother. Let one draw the other. Turn about, thou who thinkest that thou art of a superior mind and therefore canst not accept the faith." If I could only explain this whole Gospel to thee word for word, I would then scourge thy forehead and prove to thee that the faith could not be false and that Christ is thy God who is enthroned in heaven, and waits for thee. Or dost thou believe? Where are thy works? Why dost thou delay about them? Hear this: There was once a monk who spoke to a distinguished man about the faith, and got him to answer why he did not believe. He answered thus: "You yourself do not believe, for if you believed you would show other works." Therefore, to you also I say: If you believe, where are your works? Your faith is something every one knows, for every one knows that Christ was put to death by the Jews, and that everywhere men pray to Him. The whole world knows that His glory has not been spread by force and weapons, but by poor fishermen. O wise man, do you think the poor fishermen were not clever enough for this? Where they worked, there they made hearts better; where they could not work, there men remained bad; and therefore was the faith true and from God. The signs which the Lord had promised followed their teaching: in His name they drove out the devil; they spoke in new tongues; if they drank any deadly drink, they received therefrom no harm. Even if these wonders had not occurred, there would have been the wonder of wonders, that poor fishermen without any miracle could accomplish so great a work as the faith. It came from God, and so is Christ true and Christ is thy God, who is in heaven and awaits thee.

You say you believe the Gospel, but you do not believe me. But the purer anything is, so much the nearer it stands to its end and purpose. The Christian life purifies the heart, and places it very near to the truth. To the Christian life will I lead you, if you would have the knowledge of the truth. If I had wished to deceive you, why should I have given you as the chief of my gifts the means of discovering my fraud? I would be verily a fool to try to impose upon you with a falsehood which you would soon detect; only because I offered you the truth, did I call you. Come here, I fear you not; the closer you examine, the clearer the truth will become to you.

There are some, however, who are ashamed of the cross of Jesus Christ, and say: If we should believe that, we should be despised everywhere, especially by the wisest. But if you would know the truth, look only on the lives of those who would have to cry wo on their unbelief if they should be measured by deeds. If you are ashamed of the cross, the Lord was not ashamed to bear that cross for you, and to die on that cross for you. Be not ashamed of His service and of the defense of the truth. Look at the servants of the devil, who are not ashamed in the open places, in the palaces, and everywhere to speak evil and to revile us. Bear then a little shame only for your Lord; for whoever follows Him will, according to our gospel, in His name drive out the devil; that is, he will drive out his sins, and lead a virtuous life; he will drive out serpents; he will throw out the lazy who come into the houses, and say evil things under the pretense of righteousness, and so are like poisonous serpents. You will see how children can withstand them with the truth of God, and drive them away. If a believer drinks anything deadly it will not hurt him: this deadly drink is the false doctrines of the lazy, from whom, as you contend with them, a little comes also to you. But he who stands unharmed in the faith, cries to you: See that you do good; seek God's glory, not your own. He that does that is of the truth, and remains unharmed. The Lord says further of the faithful: They shall lay their hands on the sick and shall heal them. The hands are the works, and the good lay such hands on the weak that they may support them when they totter. Do I not teach you according to the Gospel? Why do you hesitate and go not into the service of the Lord? Do you ask me still what you ought to do? I will, in conclusion, tell you.

Look to Christ and you will find that all He says concerns faith. Ask the apostle; he speaks of nothing else than of faith. If you have the ground of all, if you have faith, you will always do what is good. Without faith man always falls into sin. You must seek faith in order to be good, or else your faith will become false. Christ commanded His disciples to preach the Gospel to all the world, and your wise men call a man a little world, a microcosm. So then preach to yourself, O man, woman, and child. Three parts the world has in you also. Preach first of all to your knowledge, and say to it: If you draw near this truth, you will have much faith; wherefore do you hesitate to use it? To your will, say: Thou seest that everything passes away; therefore love not the world, love Christ. Thereupon turn to the second part of your world, and say to it: Be thankful, O my memory, for the mercies God has shown thee, that thou thinkest not of the things of this world but of the mercy of thy creation, and thy redemption through the blood of the Son of God. Then go to the third part, to thy imagination, and proclaim to it: Set nothing before my eyes but my death, bring nothing before me but the Crucified, embrace Him, fly to Him. Then go through all the cities of thy world and preach to them. First say to thine eyes: Look not on vanity. To thy ears say: Listen not to the words of the lazy, but only to the words of Jesus. To thy tongue say: Speak no more evil. For thy tongue is as a great rock that rolls from the summit of a mountain, and at first falls slowly, then ever faster and more furiously. It begins with gentle murmuring, then it utters small sins, and then greater, until it finally breaks forth in open blasphemy. To thy palate say: It is necessary that we do a little penance. In all thy senses be clean, and turn to the Lord, for He it is who will give you correction and purity. To thy hands say: Do good and give alms; and let thy feet go in the good way. Our reformation has begun in the Spirit of God, if you take it to heart that each one has to preach to himself. Then will we in the name of Jesus drive out the devils of temptation. Yes, call upon Jesus as often as temptation approaches: call upon Him a hundred times and believe firmly, and the temptation will depart. Then will we speak with new tongues; we will speak with God. We shall drive away serpents; the enticement of the senses are these serpents. If we drink anything deadly it will not hurt us; if anger and lust arise in us, at the name of Jesus they will have to give way. We shall lay our hands upon the sick and heal them; with good deeds shall we strengthen the weak soul. If thou feelest thy weakness, flee to God, and He will strengthen; therefore He is thy only refuge. He is thy Savior and thy Lord, who went into the heavens to prepare a place for thee, and to wait thee there. What do you intend to do? Go and follow Jesus, who is praised from everlasting to everlasting. Amen.

LUTHER

THE METHOD AND FRUITS OF JUSTIFICATION

BIOGRAPHICAL NOTE

MARTIN LUTHER, leader of the Reformation, was born at Eisleben in 1483, and died there 1546. His rugged character and powerful intellect, combined with a strong physique, made him a natural orator, so that it was said "his words were half battles."

Of his own method of preaching he once remarked:

"When I ascend the pulpit I see no heads, but imagine those that are before me to be all blocks. When I preach I sink myself deeply down; I regard neither doctors nor masters, of which there are in the church above forty. But I have an eye to the multitude of young people, children, and servants, of which there are more than two thousand. I preach to them. When he preaches on any article a man must first distinguish it, then define, describe, and show what it is; thirdly, he must produce sentences from the Scripture to prove and to strengthen it; fourthly, he must explain it by examples; fifthly, he must adorn it with similitudes; and lastly, he must admonish and arouse the indolent, correct the disobedient, and reprove the authors of false doctrine."

LUTHER
1483—1546

THE METHOD AND FRUITS OF JUSTIFICATION

Now I say, that the heir, as long as he is a child, differeth nothing from a servant, though he be Lord of all; but is under tutors and governors until the time appointed of the father. Even so we, when we were children, were in bondage under the elements of the world: but when the fullness of the time was come, God sent forth his Son, made of a woman, made under the law, to redeem them that were under the law, that we might receive the adoption of sons. And because ye are sons, God hath sent forth the Spirit of his Son into your hearts, crying, Abba, Father. Wherefore thou art no more a servant, but a son, and if a son, then an heir of God through Christ.—Gal. iv., 1-7.

THIS text touches the very pith of Paul's chief doctrine. The cause why it is well understood but by few is, not that it is so obscure and difficult, but because there is so little knowledge of faith left in the world; without which it is not possible to understand Paul, who everywhere treats of faith with such earnestness and force. I must, therefore, speak in such a manner that this text will appear plain; and that I may more conveniently illustrate it, I will speak a few words by way of preface.

First, therefore, we must understand the doctrine in which good works are set forth, far different from that which treats of justification; as there is a great difference between the substance and its working; between man and his work. Justification pertains to man, and not to works; for man is either justified and saved, or judged and condemned, and not works. Neither is it a controversy among the godly, that man is not justified by works, but righteousness must come from some other source than from his own works: for Moses, writing of Abel, says, "The Lord had respect unto Abel, and to his offering." First, He had respect to Abel himself, then to his offering; because Abel was first counted righteous and acceptable to God, and then for his sake his offering was accepted also, and not he because of his offering. Again, God had no respect to Cain, and therefore neither to his offering: therefore thou seest that regard is had first to the worker, then to the work.

From this it is plainly gathered that no work can be acceptable to God, unless he which worketh it was first accepted by Him: and again, that no work is disallowed of Him unless the author thereof be disallowed before. I think these remarks will be sufficient concerning this matter at present, by which it is easy to understand that there are two sorts of works, those before justification and those after it; and that these last are good works indeed, but the former only appear to be good. Hereof cometh such disagreement between God and those counterfeit holy ones; for this cause nature and reason rise and rage against the Holy Ghost; this is that of which almost the whole Scripture treats. The Lord in His Word defines all works that go before justification to be evil, and of no importance, and requires that man before all things be justified. Again, He pronounces all men which are unregenerate, and have that nature which they received of their parents unchanged, to be righteous and wicked, according to that saying "all men are liars," that is, unable to perform their duty, and to do those things which they ought to do; and "Every imagination of the thoughts of his heart are only evil continually"; whereby he is able to do nothing that is good, for the fountain of his actions, which is his heart, is corrupted. If he do works which outwardly seem good, they are no better than the offering of Cain.

Here again comes forth reason, our reverend mistress, seeming to be marvelously wise, but who indeed is unwise and blind, gainsaying her God, and reproving Him of lying; being furnished with her follies and feeble honor, to wit, the light of nature, free will, the strength of nature; also with the books of the heathen and the doctrines of men, contending that the works of a man not justified are good works, and not like those of Cain, yea, and so good that he that worketh them is justified by them; that God will have respect, first to the works, then to the worker. Such doctrine now bears the sway everywhere in schools, colleges, monasteries wherein no other saints than Cain was, have rule and authority. Now from this error comes another: they which attribute so much to works, and do not accordingly esteem the worker, and sound justification, go so far that they ascribe all merit and righteousness to works done before justification, making no account of faith, alleging that which James saith, that without works faith is dead. This sentence of the apostle they do not rightly understand; making but little account of faith, they always stick to works, whereby they think to merit exceedingly, and are persuaded that for their work's sake they shall obtain the favor of God: by this means they continually disagree with God, showing themselves to be the posterity of Cain. God hath respect unto man, then unto the works of man; God alloweth the work for the sake of him that worketh, these require that for the work's sake the worker may be crowned.

But here, perhaps, thou wilt say, what is needful to be done? By what means shall I become righteous and acceptable to God? How shall I attain to this perfect justification? Those the gospel answers, teaching that it is necessary that thou hear Christ, and repose thyself wholly on Him, denying thyself and distrusting thine own strength; by this means thou shalt be changed from Cain to Abel, and being thyself acceptable, shalt offer acceptable gifts to the Lord. It is faith that justifies thee, thou being endued therewith; the Lord remitteth all thy sins by the mediation of Christ His Son, in whom this faith believeth and trusteth. Moreover, He giveth unto such a faith His Spirit, which changes the man and makes him anew, giving him another reason and another will. Such a one worketh nothing but good works. Wherefore nothing is required unto justification but to hear Jesus Christ our Savior, and to believe in Him. Howbeit these are not the works of nature, but of grace.

He, therefore, that endeavors to attain to these things by works shutteth the way to the gospel, to faith, grace, Christ, God, and all things that help unto salvation. Again, nothing is necessary in order to accomplish good works but justification; and he that hath attained it performs good works, and not any other. Hereof it sufficiently appears that the beginning, the things following, and the order of man's salvation are after this sort; first of all it is required that thou hear the Word of God; next that thou believe; then that thou work; and so at last become saved and happy. He that changes this order, without doubt is not of God. Paul also describes this, saying, "Whosoever shall call upon the name of the Lord shall be saved. How then shall they call on Him in whom they have not believed? and, how shall they believe in Him of whom they have not heard? and, how shall they hear without a preacher? and, how shall they preach except they be sent?"

Christ teaches us to pray the Lord of the harvest to send forth laborers into His harvest; that is, sincere preachers. When we hear these preach the true Word of God, we may believe; which faith justifies a man, and makes him godly indeed, so that he now calls upon God in the spirit of holiness, and works nothing but that which is good, and thus becomes a saved man. Thus he that believeth shall be saved; but he that worketh without faith is condemned; as Christ saith, he that doth not believe shall be condemned, from which no works shall deliver him. Some say, I will now endeavor to become honest. It is meet surely that we study to lead an honest life, and to do good works. But if one ask them how we may apply ourselves unto honesty, and by what means we may attain it, they answer, that we must fast, pray, frequent temples, avoid sins, etc. Whereby one becomes a Carthusian monk, another chooses some other order of monks, and another is consecrated a priest; some torment their flesh by wearing hair-cloth, others scourge their bodies with whips, others afflict themselves in a different manner; but these are of Cain's progeny, and their works are no better than his; for they continue the same that they were before, ungodly, and without justification: there is a change made of outward works only, of apparel, of place, etc.

They scarce think of faith, they presume only on such works as seem good to themselves, thinking by them to get to heaven. But Christ said, "Enter in at the strait gate, for I say unto you, many seek to enter in, and can not." Why is this? because they know not what this narrow gate is; for it is faith, which altogether annihilates or makes a man appear as nothing in his own eyes, and requires him not to trust in his own works, but to depend upon the grace of God, and be prepared to leave and suffer all things. Those holy ones of Cain's progeny think their good works are the narrow gate; and are not, therefore, extenuated or made less, whereby they might enter.

When we begin to preach of faith to those that believe altogether in works, they laugh and hiss at us, and say, "Dost thou count us as Turks and heathens, whom it behooves now first to learn faith? is there such a company of priests, monks, and nuns, and is not faith known? who knoweth not what he ought to believe? even sinners know that." Being after this sort animated and stirred up, they think themselves abundantly endued with faith, and that the rest is now to be finished and made perfect by works. They make so small and slender account of faith, because they are ignorant what faith is, and that it alone doth justify. They call it faith, believing those things which they have heard of Christ; this kind of faith the devils also have, and yet they are not justified. But this ought rather to be called an opinion of men. To believe those things to be true which are preached of Christ is not sufficient to constitute thee a Christian, but thou must not doubt that thou art of the number of them unto whom all the benefits of Christ are given and exhibited; which he that believes must plainly confess, that he is holy, godly, righteous, the son of God, and certain of salvation; and that by no merit of his own, but by the mere mercy of God poured forth upon him for Christ's sake: which he believes to be so rich and plentiful, as indeed it is, that altho he be as it were drowned in sin, he is notwithstanding made holy, and become the son of God.

Wherefore, take heed that thou nothing doubt that thou art the son of God, and therefore made righteous by His grace; let all fear and care be done away. However, thou must fear and tremble that thou mayest persevere in this way unto the end; but thou must not do this as tho it consisted in thy own strength, for righteousness and salvation are of grace, whereunto only thou must trust. But when thou knowest that it is of grace alone, and that thy faith also is the gift of God, thou shalt have cause to fear, lest some temptation violently move thee from this faith.

Every one by faith is certain of this salvation; but we ought to have care and fear that we stand and persevere, trusting in the Lord, and not in our own strength. When those of the race of Cain hear faith treated of in this manner, they marvel at our madness, as it seems to them. God turn us from this way, say they, that we should affirm ourselves holy and godly; far be this arrogance and rashness from us: we are miserable sinners; we should be mad, if we should arrogate holiness to ourselves. Thus they mock at true faith, and count such doctrine as this execrable error; and thus try to extinguish the Gospel. These are they that deny the faith of Christ, and persecute it throughout the whole world; of whom Paul speaks: "In the latter times many shall depart from the faith," etc., for we see by these means that true faith lies everywhere opprest; it is not preached, but commonly disallowed and condemned.

The pope, bishops, colleges, monasteries, and universities have more than five hundred years persecuted it with one mind and consent most obstinately, which has been the means of driving many to hell. If any object against the admiration, or rather the mad senselessness of these men, if we count ourselves even holy, trusting the goodness of God to justify us, or as David prayed, "Preserve Thou me, O Lord, for I am holy," or as Paul saith, "The Spirit of God beareth witness with our spirit that we are the children of God"; they answer that the prophet and apostle would not teach us in these words, or give us an example which we should follow, but that they, being particularly and specially enlightened, received such revelation of themselves. In this way they misrepresent the Scripture, which affirms that they are holy, saying that such doctrine is not written for us, but that it is rather peculiar miracles, which do not belong to all. This forged imagination we account of as having come from their sickly brain. Again, they believe that they shall be made righteous and holy by their own works, and that because of them God will give them salvation and eternal blessedness.

In the opinion of these men it is a Christian duty to think that we shall be righteous and sacred because of our works; but to believe that these things are given by the grace of God, they condemn as heretical; attributing that to their own works which they do not attribute to the grace of God. They that are endued with true faith, and rest upon the grace of the Lord, rejoice with holy joy, and apply themselves with pleasure to good works, not such as those of Cain's progeny do, as feigned prayers, fasting, base and filthy apparel, and such like trifles, but to true and good works whereby their neighbors are profited.

Perhaps some godly man may think, if the matter be so, and our work do not save us, to what end are so many precepts given us, and why doth God require that they be obeyed? The present text of the apostle will give a solution of this question, and upon this occasion we will give an exposition thereof. The Galatians being taught of Paul the faith of Christ, but afterward seduced by false apostles, thought that our salvation must be finished and made perfect by the works of the law; and that faith alone doth not suffice. These Paul calls back again from works unto faith with great diligence; plainly proving that the works of the law, which go before faith, make us only servants, and are of no importance toward godliness and salvation; but that faith makes us the sons of God, and from thence good works without constraint forthwith plentifully flow.

But here we must observe the words of the apostle; he calls him a servant that is occupied in works without faith, of which we have already treated at large; but he calls him a son which is righteous by faith alone. The reason is this, altho the servant apply himself to good works, yet he does it not with the same mind as doth the son; that is, with a mind free, willing, and certain that the inheritance and all the good things of the Father are his; but does it as he that is hired in another man's house, who hopes not that the inheritance shall come to him. The works indeed of the son and the servant are alike, and almost the same in outward appearance; but their minds differ exceedingly: as Christ saith, "The servant abideth not in the house forever, but the son abideth ever."

Those of Cain's progeny want the faith of sons, which they confess themselves; for they think it most absurd, and wicked arrogancy, to affirm themselves to be the sons of God, and holy; therefore as they believe, even so are they counted before God; they neither become holy nor the sons of God, nevertheless are they exercised with the works of the law; wherefore they are and remain servants forever. They receive no reward except temporal things; such as quietness of life, abundance of goods, dignity, honor, etc., which we see to be common among the followers of popish religion. But this is their reward, for they are servants, and not sons; wherefore in death they shall be separated from all good things, neither shall any portion of the eternal inheritance be theirs, who in this life would believe nothing thereof. We perceive, therefore, that servants and sons are not unlike in works, but in mind and faith they have no resemblance.

The apostle endeavors here to prove that the law with all the works thereof makes us but mere servants, if we have not faith in Christ; for this alone make us sons of God. It is the word of grace followed by the Holy Ghost, as is shown in many places, where we read of the Holy Ghost falling on Cornelius and his family while hearing the preaching of Peter. Paul teaches that no man is justified before God by the works of the law; for sin only cometh by the law. He that trusts in works condemns faith as the most pernicious arrogancy and error of all others. Here thou seest plainly that such a man is not righteous, being destitute of that faith and belief which is necessary to make him acceptable before God and His Son; yea, he is an enemy to this faith, and therefore to righteousness also. Thus it is easy to understand that which Paul saith, that no man is justified before God by the works of the law.

The worker must be justified before God before he can work any good thing. Men judge the worker by the works; God judges the works by the worker. The first precept requires us to acknowledge and worship one God, that is, to trust Him alone, which is the true faith whereby we become the sons of God. Thou canst not be delivered from the evil of unbelief by thine own power, nor by the power of the law; wherefore all thy works which thou doest to satisfy the law can be nothing but works of the law; of far less importance than to be able to justify thee before God, who counteth them righteous only who truly believe in Him; for they that acknowledge Him the true God are His sons, and do truly fulfil the law. If thou shouldst even kill thyself by working, thy heart can not obtain this faith thereby, for thy works are even a hindrance to it, and cause thee to persecute it.

He that studieth to fulfil the law without faith is afflicted for the devil's sake; and continues a persecutor both of faith and the law, until he come to himself, and cease to trust in his own works; he then gives glory to God, who justifies the ungodly, and acknowledges himself to be nothing, and sighs for the grace of God, of which he knows that he has need. Faith and grace now fill his empty mind, and satisfy his hunger; then follow works which are truly good; neither are they works of the law, but of the spirit, of faith and grace; they are called in the Scripture the works of God, which He worketh in us.

Whatsoever we do of our own power and strength, that which is not wrought in us by His grace, without doubt is a work of the law, and avails nothing toward justification; but is displeasing to God, because of the unbelief wherein it is done. He that trusts in works does nothing freely and with a willing mind; he would do no good work at all if he were not compelled by the fear of hell, or allured by the hope of present good. Whereby it is plainly seen that they strive only for gain, or are moved with fear, showing that they rather hate the law from their hearts, and had rather there were no law at all. An evil heart can do nothing that is good. This evil propensity of the heart, and unwillingness to do good, the law betrays when it teaches that God does not esteem the works of the hand, but those of the heart.

Thus sin is known by the law, as Paul teaches; for we learn thereby that our affections are not placed on that which is good. This ought to teach us not to trust in ourselves, but to long after the grace of God, whereby the evil of the heart may be taken away, and we become ready to do good works, and love the law voluntarily; not for fear of any punishment, but for the love of righteousness. By this means one is made of a servant, a son; of a slave an heir.

We shall now come to treat more particularly of the text. Verse 1. "The heir, as long as he is a child, differeth nothing from a servant, tho he be lord of all." We see that the children unto whom their parents have left some substance are brought up no otherwise than if they were servants. They are fed and clothed with their goods, but they are not permitted to do with them, nor use them according to their own minds, but are ruled with fear and discipline of manners, so that even in their own inheritance they live no otherwise than as servants. After the same sort it is in spiritual things. God made with His people a covenant, when He promised that in the seed of Abraham, that is in Christ, all nations of the earth should be blest. That covenant was afterward confirmed by the death of Christ, and revealed and published abroad by the preaching gospel. For the gospel is an open and general preaching of this grace, that in Christ is laid up a blessing for all men that believe.

Before this covenant is truly opened and made manifest to men, the sons of God live after the manner of servants under the law; and are exercised with the works of the law, altho they can not be justified by them; they are true heirs of heavenly things, of this blessing and grace of the covenant; altho they do not as yet know or enjoy it. Those that are justified by grace cease from the works of the law, and come unto the inheritance of justification; they then freely work those things that are good, to the glory of God and benefit of their neighbors. For they have possest it by the covenant of the Father, confirmed by Christ, revealed, published, and as it were delivered into their hands by the gospel, through the grace and mercy of God.

This covenant Abraham, and all the fathers which were endued with true faith, had no otherwise than we have: altho before Christ was glorified this grace was not openly preached and published: they lived in like faith, and therefore obtained the like good things. They had the same grace, blessing, and covenant that we have; for there is one Father and God over all. Thou seest that Paul here, as in almost all other places, treats much of faith; that we are not justified by works, but by faith alone. There is no good thing which is not contained in this covenant of God; it gives righteousness, salvation, and peace. By faith the whole inheritance of God is at once received. From thence good works come; not meritorious, whereby thou mayest seek salvation, but which with a mind already possessing righteousness thou must do with great pleasure to the profit of thy neighbors.

Verse 2. "But is under tutors and governors until the time appointed of the Father." Tutors and governors are they which bring up the heir, and so rule him and order his goods that he neither waste his inheritance by riotous living, nor his goods perish or be otherwise consumed. They permit him not to use his goods at his own will or pleasure, but suffer him to enjoy them as they shall be needful and profitable to him. They keep him at home, and instruct him whereby he may long and comfortably enjoy his inheritance: but as soon as he arrives to the years of discretion and judgment, it can not but be grievous to him to live in subjection to the commands and will of another.

In the same manner stands the case of the children of God, which are brought up and instructed under the law, as under a master in the liberty of sons. The law profits them in this, that by the fear of it and the punishment which it threatens, they are driven from sin, at least from the outward work: by it they are brought to a knowledge of themselves, and that they do no good at all with a willing and ready mind as becomes sons; whereby they may easily see what is the root of this evil, and what is especially needful unto salvation; to wit, a new and living spirit to that which is good: which neither the law nor the works of the law is able to give; yea, the more they apply themselves to it, the more unwilling they find themselves to work those things which are good.

Here they learn that they do not satisfy the law, altho outwardly they live according to its precepts. They pretend to obey it in works, altho in mind they hate it; they pretend themselves righteous, but they remain sinners. These are like unto those of Cain's progeny, and hypocrites; whose hands are compelled to do good, but their hearts consent unto sin and are subject thereto. To know this concerning one's self is not the lowest degree toward salvation. Paul calls such constrained works the works of the law; for they flow not from a ready and willing heart; howbeit the law does not require works alone, but the heart itself; wherefore it is said in the first psalm of the blest man, "But his delight is in the law of the Lord: and in His law doth he meditate day and night." Such a mind the law requires, but it gives it not; neither can it of its own nature: whereby it comes to pass that while the law continues to exact it of a man, and condemns him as long as he hath such a mind, as being disobedient to God, he is in anguish on every side; his conscience being grievously terrified.

Then, indeed, is he most ready to receive the grace of God; this being the time appointed by the Father when his servitude shall end, and he enter into the liberty of the sons of God. For being thus in distress, and terrified, seeing that by no other means he can avoid the condemnation of the law, he prays to the Father for grace; he acknowledges his frailty, he confesses his sin, he ceases to trust in works, and humbles himself, perceiving that between him and a manifest sinner there is no difference at all except of works, that he hath a wicked heart, even as every other sinner hath. The condition of man's nature is such that it is able to give to the law works only, and not the heart; an unequal division, truly, to dedicate the heart, which, incomparably excels all other things, to sin, and the hand to the law: which is offering chaff to the law, and the wheat to sin; the shell to God, and the kernel to Satan; whose ungodliness if one reprove, they become enraged, and would even take the life of innocent Abel, and persecute all those that follow the truth.

Those that trust in works seem to defend them to obtain righteousness; they promise to themselves a great reward for this, by persecuting heretics and blasphemers, as they say, who seduce with error, and entice many from good works. But those that God hath chosen, learn by the law how unwilling the heart is to conform to the works of the law; they fall from their arrogancy, and are by this knowledge of themselves brought to see their own unworthiness. Hereby they receive that covenant of the eternal blessing and the

Holy Ghost which renews the heart: whereby they are delighted with the law, and hate sin; and are willing and ready to do those things which are good. This is the time appointed by the Father, when the heir must no longer remain a servant, but a son; being led by a free spirit, he is no more kept in subjection under tutors and governors after the manner of a servant; which is even that which Paul teaches in the following:

Verse 3. "Even so we, when we were children, were in bondage under the elements of the word." By the word elements thou mayest here understand the first principles or law written; which is as it were the first exercises and instructions of holy learning; as it is said: "As concerning the time ye ought to be teachers, ye have need that one teach you again which be the first principles of the oracles of God." "Beware lest any man spoil you through philosophy and vain deceit, after the tradition of men, after the rudiments of the world." "How turn ye again to the weak and beggarly elements, whereunto ye desire again to be in bondage."

Here Paul calls the law rudiments; because it is not able to perform that righteousness which it requires. For whereas it earnestly requires a heart and mind given to godliness, nature is not able to satisfy it: herein it makes a man feel his poverty, and acknowledge his infirmity: it requires that of him by right which he has not, neither is able to have. "The letter killeth, but the Spirit giveth life." Paul calls them the rudiments of the world, which, not being renewed by the Spirit, only perform worldly things; to wit, in places, times, apparel, persons, vessels, and such like. But faith rests not in worldly things, but in the grace, word, and mercy of God: counting alike, days, meats, persons, apparel, and all things of this world.

None of these by themselves either help or hinder godliness or salvation. With those of Cain's progeny, faith neither agrees in name or anything else; one of them eats flesh, another abstains from it; one wears black apparel, another white; one keeps this day holy, and another that; every one has his rudiments, under which he is in bondage: all of them are addicted to the things of the world, which are frail and perishable. Against these Paul speaks, "Wherefore, if ye be dead with Christ from the rudiments of the world, why, as tho living in the world, are ye subject to ordinances: touch not, taste not, handle not, which all are to perish with the using, after the commandments and doctrines of men? Which things have indeed a show of wisdom in will-worship and humility, and neglecting of the body; not in any honor to the satisfying of the flesh."

By this and other places above mentioned,

it is evident that monasteries and colleges, whereby we measure the state of spiritual men as we call them, plainly disagree with the Gospel and Christian liberty: and therefore it is much more dangerous to live in this kind of life than among the most profane men. All their works are nothing but rudiments and ordinances of the world; neither are they Christians but in name, wherefore all their life and holiness are sinful and most detestable hypocrisy. The fair show of feigned holiness which is in those ordinances does, in a marvelous and secret manner, withdraw from faith more than those manifest and gross sins of which open sinners are guilty. Now this false and servile opinion faith alone takes away, and teaches us to trust in, and rest upon, the grace of God, whereby is given freely that which is needful to work all things.

Verse 4. "But when the fulness of the time was come, God sent forth His Son, made of a woman, made under the law, to redeem them that were under the law, that we might receive the adoption of sons." After Paul had taught us that righteousness and faith can not come to us by the law, neither can we deserve it by nature, he shows us by whom we obtain it; and who is the author of our justification. The apostle saith, "When the fulness of the time was come"; here Paul speaks of the time which was appointed by the Father to the Son, wherein He should live under tutors, etc. This time being come to the Jews, and ended, Christ came in the flesh; so it is daily fulfilled to others, when they come to the knowledge of Christ, and change the servitude of the law for the faith of sons. Christ for this cause came unto us, that believing in Him we may be restored to true liberty; by which faith they of ancient times also obtained the liberty of the Spirit.

As soon as thou believest in Christ, He comes to thee, a deliverer and Savior; and now the time of bondage is ended; as the apostle saith, the fulness thereof is come.

Verse 6. "And because ye are sons, God hath sent forth the Spirit of His Son into your hearts, crying, Abba, Father." Here we see plainly that the Holy Ghost cometh to the saints, not by works, but by faith alone. Sons believe, while servants only work; sons are free from the law, servants are held under the law, as appears by those things that have been before spoken. But how comes it to pass that he saith "because ye are sons, God hath sent forth the Spirit," etc., seeing it is before said that by the coming of the Spirit we are changed from servants to sons: but here, as tho we could be sons before the coming of the Spirit, he saith "because ye are sons," etc. To this question we must answer, that Paul speaks here in the same manner that he did before, that is, before the fulness of the time came, we were in bondage under the rudiments of the world: all that shall become sons are counted in the place of sons with God: therefore he saith rightly, "because ye are sons," that is, because the state of sons is appointed to you from everlasting, "God hath sent forth the Spirit of His Son," to wit, that He might finish it in you, and make you such as He hath long since of His goodness determined that He would make you.

Now if the Father give unto us His Spirit, He will make us His true sons and heirs, that we may with confidence cry with Christ, Abba, Father; being His brethren and fellow heirs. The apostle has well set forth the goodness of God which makes us partakers with Christ, and causes us to have all things common with Him, so that we live and are led by the same Spirit. These words of the apostle show that the Holy Ghost proceeds from Christ, as he calls Him his Spirit. So God hath sent forth the Spirit of His Son, that is, of Christ, for He is the Spirit of God, and comes from God to us, and not ours, unless one will say after this manner, "my Holy Spirit," as we say, "my God," "my Lord," etc. As He is said to be the Holy Spirit of Christ, it proves Him to be God of whom that Spirit is sent, therefore it is counted His Spirit.

Christians may perceive by this whether they have in themselves the Holy Ghost, to wit, the Spirit of sons; whether they hear His voice in their hearts: for Paul saith, He crieth in the hearts which He possesseth, Abba, Father; he saith also, "We have received the Spirit of adoption, whereby we cry Abba, Father." Thou hearest this voice when thou findest so much faith in thyself that thou dost assuredly, without doubting, presume that not only thy sins are forgiven thee, but also that thou art the beloved Son of God, who, being certain of eternal salvation, durst both call Him Father, and be delighted in Him with a joyful and confident heart. To doubt these things brings a reproach upon the death of Christ, as tho He had not obtained all things for us.

It may be that thou shalt be so tempted as to fear and doubt, and think plainly that God is not a favorable Father, but a wrathful revenger of sins, as it happened with Job, and many other saints: but in such a conflict this trust and confidence that thou art a son ought to prevail and overcome. It is said "The Spirit itself maketh intercession for us with groanings which can not be uttered; and that He beareth witness with our spirit that we are the children of God." How can it therefore be that our hearts should not hear this cry and testimony of the Spirit? But if thou dost not feel this cry, take heed that thou be not slothful and secure; pray constantly, for thou art in an evil state.

Cain saith, "My punishment is greater than I can bear. Behold, Thou hast driven me out this day from the face of the earth, and from Thy face shall I be hid; and it shall come to pass that every one that findeth me shall slay me." This is a dreadful and terrible cry, which is heard from all Cain's progeny, all such as trust to themselves and their own works, who put not their trust in the Son of God, neither consider that He was sent from the Father, made of a woman under the law, much less that all these things were done for their salvation. And while their ungodliness is not herewith content, they begin to persecute even the sons of God, and grow so cruel that, after the example of their father Cain, they can not rest until they slay their righteous brother Abel, wherefore the blood of Christ continually cries out against them nothing but punishment and vengeance; but for the heirs of salvation it cries by the Spirit of Christ for nothing but grace and reconciliation.

The apostle here uses a Syrian and Greek word, saying, Abba, Pater. This word Abba, in the Syrian tongue, signifies a father, by which name the heads of monasteries are still called; and by the same name, hermits in times past, being holy men, called their presidents: at last, by use, it was also made a Latin word. Therefore that which Paul saith is as much as Father, Father; or if thou hadst rather, "my Father."

Verse 7. "Wherefore thou art no more a servant, but a son, and if a son, then an heir of God through Christ." He saith, that after the coming of the Spirit, after the knowledge of Christ, "thou art not a servant." A son is free and willing, a servant is compelled and unwilling; a son liveth and resteth in faith, a servant in works. Therefore it appears that we can not obtain salvation of God by works, but before thou workest that which is acceptable to Him, it is necessary that thou receive salvation; then good works will freely flow, to the honor of thy heavenly Father, and to the profit of thy neighbors; without any fear of punishment, or looking for reward.

If this inheritance of the Father be thine by faith, surely thou art rich in all things, before thou hast wrought any thing. It is said "Your salvation is prepared and reserved in heaven, to be showed in the last time," wherefore the works of a Christian ought to have no regard to merit, which is the manner of servants, but only for the use and benefit of our neighbors, whereby we may truly live to the glory of God. Lest that any think that so great an inheritance cometh to us without cost (altho it be given to us without our cost or merit), yet it cost Christ a dear price, who, that He might purchase it for us, was made under the law, and satisfied it for us, both by life and also by death.

Those benefits which from love we bestow upon our neighbor, come to him freely, without any charges or labor of his, notwithstanding they cost us something, even as Christ hath bestowed those things which are His upon us. Thus hath Paul called back the Galatians from the teachers of works, which preached nothing but the law, perverting the Gospel of Christ. Which things are very necessary to be marked of us also: for the Pope, with his prelates and monks hath for a long time intruded, urging his laws, which are foolish and pernicious, disagreeing in every respect with the Word of God, seducing almost the whole world from the gospel of Christ, and plainly extinguishing the faith of sons, as the Scripture hath in diverse places manifestly prophesied of His kingdom. Wherefore let every one that desires salvation, diligently take heed of him and his followers, no otherwise than Satan himself.

LATIMER

ON CHRISTIAN LOVE

BIOGRAPHICAL NOTE

HUGH LATIMER, reformer and martyr, was born in Leicestershire, England, in 1485, or two years later than Luther. On completing an education at Cambridge, he took holy orders and preached strenuously in favor of the Lutheran views. As a profound canonist, he was placed on the commission appointed to decide on the legality of Henry VIII's marriage with Katharine of Aragon. His decision in favor of Henry gained him a royal chaplaincy and a living.

Appointed Bishop of Worcester in 1535, he preached boldly the reformed doctrines, but lost favor at court, and when Gardiner and Bonner pushed a reactionary movement to the front, he retired from his see (1539). Latimer lived in peaceful retirement under Edward VI, but under Mary he, with other reformers, was arrested and thrown into the Tower. Brought to Oxford for examination, he refused to recant, and was confined for a year in the common prison, and on October 16, 1555, put to death by fire, along with Ridley, at a place opposite Balliol College, where the Martyr's Memorial was subsequently erected.

LATIMER
1485—1555

ON CHRISTIAN LOVE

This is my commandment, that ye love one another, as I have loved you.—John xv., 12.

SEEING the time is so far spent, we will take no more in hand at this time than this one sentence; for it will be enough for us to consider this well, and to bear it away with us. "This I command unto you, that ye love one another." Our Savior himself spake these words at His last supper: it was the last sermon that He made unto His disciples before His departure; it is a very long sermon. For our Savior, like as one that knows he shall die shortly, is desirous to spend that little time that He has with His friends, in exhorting and instructing them how they should lead their lives. Now among other things that He commanded this was one: "This I command unto you, that ye love one another." The English expresses as tho it were but one, "This is my commandment." I examined the Greek, where it is in the plural number, and very well; for there are many things that pertain to a Christian man, and yet all those things are contained in this one thing, that is, love. He lappeth up all things in love.

Our whole duty is contained in these words, "Love together." Therefore St. Paul saith, "He that loveth another fulfilleth the whole law"; so it appeareth that all things are contained in this word love. This love is a precious thing; our Savior saith, "By this shall all men know that ye are my disciples, if ye shall love one another."

So Christ makes love His cognizance, His badge, His livery. Like as every lord commonly gives a certain livery to his servants, whereby they may be known that they pertain unto him; and so we say, yonder is this lord's servants, because they wear his livery: so our Savior, who is the Lord above all lords, would have His servants known by their liveries and badge, which badge is love alone. Whosoever now is endued with love and charity is His servant; him we may call Christ's servant; for love is the token whereby you may know that such a servant pertaineth to Christ; so that charity may be called the very livery of Christ. He that hath charity is Christ's servant; he that hath not charity is the servant of the devil. For as Christ's livery is love and charity, so the devil's livery is hatred, malice and discord.

But I think the devil has a great many more servants than Christ has; for there are a great many more in his livery than in

Christ's livery; there are but very few who are endued with Christ's livery; with love and charity, gentleness and meekness of spirit; but there are a great number that bear hatred and malice in their hearts, that are proud, stout, and lofty; therefore the number of the devil's servants is greater than the number of Christ's servants.

Now St. Paul shows how needful this love is. I speak not of carnal love, which is only animal affection; but of this charitable love, which is so necessary that when a man hath it, without all other things it will suffice him. Again, if a man have all other things and lacketh that love it will not help him, it is all vain and lost. St. Paul used it so: "Tho I speak with tongues of men and angels, and yet had no love, I were even as sounding brass, or as a tinkling cymbal. And tho I could prophesy and understand all secrets and all knowledge; yet if I had faith, so that I could move mountains out of their places, and yet had no love, I were nothing. And tho I bestowed all my goods to feed the poor, and tho I gave my body even that I were burned, and yet had no love, it profiteth me nothing" (I Cor. xiii). These are godly gifts, yet St. Paul calls them nothing when a man hath them without charity; which is a great commendation, and shows the great need of love, insomuch that all other virtues are in vain when this love is absent. And there have been some who taught that St. Paul spake against the dignity of faith; but you must understand that St. Paul speaks here not of the justifying faith, wherewith we receive everlasting life, but he understands by this word faith the gift to do miracles, to remove hills; of such a faith he speaks. This I say to confirm this proposition. Faith only justifieth; this proposition is most true and certain. And St. Paul speaks not here of this lively justifying faith; for this right faith is not without love, for love cometh and floweth out of faith; love is a child of faith; for no man can love except he believe, so that they have two several offices, they themselves being inseparable.

St. Paul has an expression in the 13th chapter of the first of the Corinthians, which, according to the outward letter, seems much to the dispraise of this faith, and to the praise of love; these are his words, "Now abideth faith, hope and love, even these three; but the chiefest of these is love." There are some learned men who expound the greatness of which St. Paul speaketh here as if meant for eternity. For when we come to God, then we believe no more, but rather see with our eyes face to face how He is; yet for all that love remains still; so that love may be called the chiefest, because she endureth forever. And tho she is the chiefest, yet we must not attribute unto her the office which pertains unto faith only. Like as I can not say, the Mayor of Stamford must make me a pair of shoes because he is a greater man than the shoemaker is; for the mayor, tho he is a greater man, yet it is not his office to make shoes; so tho love be greater, yet it is not her office to save. Thus much I thought good to say against those who fight against the truth.

Now, when we would know who are in Christ's livery or not, we must learn it of St. Paul, who most evidently described charity, which is the only livery, saying, "Love is patient, she suffereth long." Now whosoever fumeth and is angry, he is out of this livery: therefore let us remember that we do not cast away the livery of Christ our Master. When we are in sickness, or any manner of adversities, our duty is to be patient, to suffer willingly, and to call upon Him for aid, help and comfort; for without Him we are not able to abide any tribulation. Therefore we must call upon God, He has promised to help: therefore let me not think Him to be false or untrue to His promises, for we can not dishonor God more than by not believing or trusting in Him. Therefore let us beware above all things of dishonoring God; and so we must be patient, trusting and most certainly believing that He will deliver us when it seems good to Him, who knows the time better than we ourselves.

"Charity is gentle, friendly, and loving;

she envieth not." They that envy their neighbor's profit when it goes well with him, such fellows are out of their liveries, and so out of the service of God; for to be envious is to be the servant of the devil.

"Love doth not frowardly, she is not a provoker"; as there are some men who will provoke their neighbor so far that it is very hard for them to be in charity with them; but we must wrestle with our affections; we must strive and see that we keep this livery of Christ our master; for "the devil goeth about as a roaring lion seeking to take us at a vantage," to bring us out of our liveries, and to take from us the knot of love and charity.

"Love swelleth not, is not puffed up"; but there are many swellers nowadays, they are so high, so lofty, insomuch that they despise and contemn all others; all such persons are under the governance of the devil. God rules not them with His good spirit; the evil spirit has occupied their hearts and possest them.

"She doth not dishonestly; she seeketh not her own; she doth all things to the commodity of her neighbors." A charitable man will not promote himself with the damage of his neighbor. They that seek only their own advantage, forgetting their neighbors, they are not of God, they have not His livery. Further, "Charity is not provoked to anger; she thinketh not evil." We ought not to think evil of our neighbor, as long as we see not open wickedness; for it is written, "You shall not judge"; we should not take upon us to condemn our neighbor. And surely the condemners of other men's works are not in the livery of Christ. Christ hateth them.

"She rejoiceth not in iniquity"; she loveth equity and godliness. And again, she is sorry to hear of falsehood, of stealing, or such like, which wickedness is now at this time commonly used. There never was such falsehood among Christian men as there is now, at this time; truly I think, and they that have experience report it so, that among the very infidels and Turks there is more fidelity and uprightness than among Christian men. For no man setteth anything by his promise, yea, and writings will not serve with some, they are so shameless that they dare deny their own handwriting; but, I pray you, are those false fellows in the livery of Christ? Have they His cognizance? No, no; they have the badge of the devil, with whom they shall be damned world without end, except they amend and leave their wickedness.

"She suffereth all things; she believeth all things." It is a great matter that should make us to be grieved with our neighbor; we should be patient when our neighbor doth wrong, we should admonish him of his folly, earnestly desiring him to leave his wickedness, showing the danger that follows, everlasting damnation. In such wise we should study to amend our neighbor, and not to hate him or do him a foul turn again, but rather charitably study to amend him: whosoever now does so, he has the livery and cognizance of Christ, he shall be known at the last day for his servant.

"Love believeth all things"; it appears daily that they who are charitable and friendly are most deceived; because they think well of every man, they believe every man, they trust their words, and therefore are most deceived in this world, among the children of the devil. These and such like things are the tokens of the right and godly love; therefore they that have this love are soon known, for this love can not be hid in corners, she has her operation: therefore all that have her are well enough, tho they have no other gifts besides her. Again, they that lack her, tho they have many other gifts besides, yet is it to no other purpose, it does then no good: for when we shall come at the great day before him, not having this livery (that is love) with us, then we are lost; he will not take us for His servants, because we have not His cognizance. But if we have this livery, if we wear His cognizance here in this world; that is, if we love our neighbor, help him in his distress, are charitable, loving, and friendly unto him, then we shall be known at the last day: but if we be uncharitable toward our neighbor, hate him, seek our own advantage with His damage, then we shall be rejected of Christ and so damned world without end.

Our Savior saith here in this gospel, "I command you these things"; He speaketh in the plural number, and lappeth it up in one thing, which is that we should love one another, much like St. Paul's saying in the 13th to the Romans, "Owe nothing to any man, but to love one another. Here St. Paul lappeth up all things together, signifying unto us that love is the consummation of the law; for this commandment, "Thou shalt not commit adultery," is contained in this law of love: for he that loveth God will not break wedlock, because wedlock-breaking is a dishonoring of God and a serving of the devil. "Thou shalt not kill"; he that loveth will not kill, he will do no harm. "Thou shalt not steal"; he that loveth his neighbor as himself will not take away his goods. I had of late occasion to speak of picking and stealing, where I showed unto you the danger wherein they are that steal their neighbor's goods from them, but I hear nothing yet of restitution. Sirs, I tell you, except restitution is made, look for no salvation. And it is a miserable and heinous thing to consider that we are so blinded with this world that, rather than we would make restitution, we will sell unto the devil our souls which are bought with the blood of our Savior Christ. What can be done more to the dishonoring of Christ than to cast our souls away to the devil for the value of a little money?—the soul which He has bought with His painful passion and death. But I tell you those that will do so, and that will not make restitution when they have done wrong, or taken away their neighbor's goods, they are not in the livery of Christ, they are not his servants; let them go as they will in this world, yet for all that they are foul and filthy enough before God; they stink before His face; and therefore they shall be cast from His presence into everlasting fire; this shall be all their good cheer that they shall have, because they have not the livery of Christ, nor His cognizance, which is love. They remember not that Christ commanded us, saying, "This I command you, that ye love one another." This is Christ's commandment. Moses, the great prophet of God, gave many laws, but he gave not the spirit to fulfil the same laws: but Christ gave this law, and promised unto us, that when we call upon Him He will give us His Holy Ghost, who shall make us able to fulfil His laws, tho not so perfectly as the law requires; but yet to the contention of God, and to the protection of our faith: for as long as we are in this world, we can do nothing as we ought to do, because our flesh leadeth us, which is ever bent against the law of God;

LATIMER

yet our works which we do are well taken for Christ's sake, and God will reward them in heaven.

Therefore our Savior saith, "my yoke is easy, and my burden is light," because He helpeth to bear them; else indeed we should not be able to bear them. And in another place He saith, "His commandments are not heavy"; they are heavy to our flesh, but being qualified with the Spirit of God, to the faithful which believe in Christ, to them, I say, they are not heavy; for tho their doings are not perfect, yet they are well taken for Christ's sake.

You must not be offended because the Scripture commends love so highly, for he that commends the daughter commends the mother; for love is the daughter, and faith is the mother: love floweth out of faith; where faith is, there is love; but yet we must consider their offices, faith is the hand wherewith we take hold on everlasting life.

Now let us enter into ourselves, and examine our own hearts, whether we are in the livery of God, or not: and when we find ourselves to be out of this livery, let us repent and amend our lives, so that we may come again to the favor of God, and spend our time in this world to His honor and glory, forgiving our neighbors all such things as they have done against us.

And now to make an end: mark here who

gave this precept of love—Christ our Savior Himself. When and at what time? At His departing, when He should suffer death. Therefore these words ought the more to be regarded, seeing He Himself spake them at His last departing from us. May God of His mercy give us grace so to walk here in this world, charitably and friendly one with another, that we may attain the joy which God hath prepared for all those that love Him. Amen.

MELANCHTHON

THE SAFETY OF THE VIRTUOUS

BIOGRAPHICAL NOTE

PHILIP MELANCHTHON (Schwarzerd) was born at Bretten, in Baden, in 1497. His name is noteworthy as first a fellow laborer and eventually a controversial antagonist of Luther. At the Diet of Augsburg, in 1530, he was the leading representative of the Reformation. He formulated the twenty-eight articles of the evangelical faith known as the "Augsburg Confession." The Lutherans of extreme Calvinistic views were alienated by Melanchthon's subsequent modifications of this confession, and by his treatises in ethics. He and his followers were bitterly assailed, but his irenic spirit did not forsake him. He was a true child of the Renaissance, and is styled by some writers "the founder of general learning throughout Europe." While he was never called or ordained to the ministry of the Church, he was in the habit of addressing the local religious assemblies or collegia from time to time, and, being a man of profound piety, his sympathetic and natural style of delivery made him an impressive speaker. He died in 1560, and his body was laid beside that of Martin Luther.

MELANCHTHON
1497—1560

THE SAFETY OF THE VIRTUOUS

Neither shall any man pluck them out of my hand.
—John x., 28.

To Thee, almighty and true God, eternal Father of our Lord Jesus Christ, maker of heaven and earth, and of all creatures, together with Thy Son our Lord Jesus Christ, and the Holy Ghost—to Thee, the wise, good, true, righteous, compassionate, pure, gracious God, we render thanks that Thou hast hitherto upheld the Church in these lands, and graciously afforded it protection and care, and we earnestly beseech Thee evermore to gather among us an inheritance for Thy Son, which may praise Thee to all eternity.

I have in these, our assemblies, often uttered partly admonitions and partly reproofs, which I hope the most of you will bear in mind. But since I must presume that now the hearts of all are wrung with a new grief and a new pang by reason of the war in our neighborhood, this season seems to call for a word of consolation. And, as we commonly say, "Where the pain is there one claps his hand," I could not, in this so great affliction, make up my mind to turn my discourse upon any other subject. I do not, indeed, doubt that you yourselves seek comfort in the divine declarations, yet will I also bring before you some things collected therefrom, because always that on which we had ourselves thought becomes more precious to us when we hear that it proves itself salutary also to others. And because long discourses are burdensome in time of sorrow and mourning, I will, without delay, bring forward that comfort which is the most effectual.

Our pains are best assuaged when something good and beneficial, especially some help toward a happy issue, presents itself. All other topics of consolation, such as men borrow from the unavoidableness of suffering, and the examples of others, bring us no great alleviation. But the Son of God, our Lord Jesus Christ, who was crucified for us and raised again, and now sits at the right hand of the Father, offers us help and deliverance, and has manifested this disposition in many declarations. I will now speak of the words: "No man shall pluck my sheep out of my hand." This expression has often raised me up out of the deepest sorrow, and drawn me, as it were, out of hell.

The wisest men in all times have bewailed the great amount of human misery which we see with our eyes before we pass into eternity —diseases, death, want, our own errors, by which we bring harm and punishment on ourselves, hostile men, unfaithfulness on the part of those with whom we are closely connected, banishment, abuse, desertion, miserable children, public and domestic strife, wars, murder, and devastation. And since such things appear to befall good and bad without distinction, many wise men have inquired whether there were any Providence, or whether accident brings everything to pass independent of a divine purpose? But we in the Church know that the first and principal cause of human wo is this, that on account of sin man is made subject to death and other calamity, which is so much more vehement in the Church, because the devil, from the hatred toward God, makes fearful assaults on the Church and strives to destroy it utterly.

Therefore it is written: "I will put enmity between the serpent and the seed of the woman." And Peter says: "Your adversary, the devil, as a roaring lion, walketh about and seeketh whom he may devour."

Not in vain, however, has God made known to us the causes of our misery. We should not only consider the greatness of our necessity, but also discern the causes of it, and recognize His righteous anger against sin, to the end that we may, on the other hand, perceive the Redeemer and the greatness of His compassion; and as witnesses to these, His declarations, He adds the raising of dead men to life, and other miracles.

Let us banish from our hearts, therefore, the unbelieving opinions which imagine that evils befall us by mere chance, or from physical causes.

But when thou considerest the wounds in thy own circle of relations, or dost cast a glance at the public disorders in the State, which again afflict the individual also (as Solon says: "The general corruption penetrates even to thy quiet habitation"), then think, first, of thy own and others' sins, and of the righteous wrath of God; and, secondly, weigh the rage of the devil, who lets loose his hate chiefly in the Church.

In all men, even the better class, great darkness reigns. We see not how great an evil sin is, and regard not ourselves as so shamefully defiled. We flatter ourselves, in particular, because we profess a better doctrine concerning God. Nevertheless, we resign ourselves to a careless slumber, or pamper each one his own desires; our impurity, the disorders of the Church, the necessity of brethren, fills us not with pain; devotion is without fire and fervor; zeal for doctrine and discipline languishes, and not a few are my sins, and thine, and those of many others, by reason of which such punishments are heaped upon us.

Let us, therefore, apply our hearts to repentance, and direct our eyes to the Son of

God, in respect to whom we have the assurance that, after the wonderful counsel of God, He is placed over the family of man, to be the protector and preserver of his Church.

We perceive not fully either of our wretchedness or our dangers, or the fury of enemies, until after events of extraordinary sorrowfulness. Still we ought to reflect thus: there must exist great need and a fearful might and rage of enemies, since so powerful a protector has been given to us, even God's Son. When He says: "No man shall pluck my sheep out of my hand," He indicates that He is no idle spectator of wo, but that mighty and incessant strife is going on. The devil incites his tools to disturb the Church or the political commonwealth, that boundless confusion may enter, followed by heathenish desolation. But the Son of God, who holds in His hands, as it were, the congregation of those who call upon His name, hurls back the devils by His infinite power, conquers and chases them thence, and will one day shut them up in the prison of hell, and punish them to all eternity with fearful pains. This comfort we must hold fast in regard to the entire Church, as well as each in regard to himself.

If, in these distracted and warring times, we see States blaze up and fall to ruin, then look away to the Son of God, who stands in the secret counsel of the Godhead and guards His little flock and carries the weak lambs, as it were, in His own hands. Be persuaded that by Him thou also shalt be protected and upheld.

Here some, not rightly instructed, will exclaim: "Truly I could wish to commend myself to such a keeper, but only His sheep does He preserve. Whether I also am counted in that flock, I know not." Against this doubt we must most strenuously contend, for the Lord Himself assures us in this very passage, that all who "hear and with faith receive the voice of the gospel are His sheep"; and He says expressly: "If a man love me, he will keep my words, and my Father will love him, and we will come to him and make our abode with him." These promises of the Son of God, which can not be shaken, we must confidently appropriate to ourselves. Nor shouldst thou, by thy doubts, exclude thyself from this blest flock, which originates in the righteousness of the gospel. They do not rightly distinguish between the law and the gospel, who, because they are unworthy, reckon not themselves among the sheep. Rather is this consolation afforded us, that we are accepted "for the Son of God's sake," truly, without merit, not on account of our own righteousness, but through faith, because we are unworthy, and impure, and far from having fulfilled the law of God. That is, moreover, a universal promise, in which the Son of God saith: "Come unto me, all ye that labor and are heavy laden, and I will give you rest."

The eternal Father earnestly commands that we should hear the Son, and it is the greatest of all transgressions if we despise Him and do not approve His voice. This is what every one should often and diligently consider, and in this disposition of the Father, revealed through the Son, find grace.

Altho, amid so great disturbances, many a sorrowful spectacle meets thine eye, and the Church is rent by discord and hate, and manifold and domestic public necessity is added thereto, still let not despair overcome thee, but know thou that thou hast the Son of God for a keeper and protector, who will not suffer either the Church, or thee, or thy family, to be plucked out of His hand by the fury of the devil.

With all my heart, therefore, do I supplicate the Son of God, our Lord Jesus Christ, who, having been crucified for us, and raised again, sits at the right hand of the Father, to bless men with His gifts, and to Him I pray that He would protect and govern this little church and me therein. Other sure trust, in this great flame when the whole world is on fire, I discern nowhere. Each one has his separate hopes, and each one with his understanding seeks to repose in something else; but however good that may all be, it is still a far better, and unquestionably a more effectual, consolation to flee to the Son of God and expect help and deliverances from Him.

Such wishes will not be in vain. For to this end are we laden with such a crowd of dangers, that in events and occurrences which to human prudence are an inexplicable enigma, we may recognize the infinite goodness and presentness of God, in that He, for His Son's sake, and through His Son, affords us aid. God will be owned in such deliverance just as in the deliverance of your first parents, who, after the fall, when they were forsaken by all the creatures, were upheld by the help of God alone. So was the family of Noah in the flood, so were the Israelites preserved when in the Red Sea they stood between the towering walls of waters. These glorious examples are held up before us, that we might know, in like manner, the Church, without the help of any created beings, is often preserved. Many in all times have experienced such divine deliverance and support in their personal dangers, as David saith: "My father and my mother have forsaken me, but the Lord taketh me up"; and in another place David saith: "He hath delivered the wretched, who hath no helper." But in order that we may become partakers of these so great blessings, faith and devotion must be kindled within us, as it stands written, "Verily, I say unto you!" So likewise must our faith be exercised, that before deliverance we should pray for help and wait for it, resting in God with a certain cheerfulness of soul; and that we should not cherish continual doubt and melancholy murmuring in our hearts, but constantly set before our eyes the admonition of God: "The peace of God which passeth all understanding keep your heart and mind"; which is to say, be so comforted in God, in time of danger, that your hearts, having been strengthened by confidence in the pity and presentness of God, may patiently wait for help and deliverance, and quietly maintain that peaceful serenity which is the beginning of eternal life, and without which there can be no true devotion.

For distrust and doubt produce a gloomy and terrible hate toward God, and that is the beginning of the eternal torments, and a rage like that of the devil.

Now you must guard against these billows in the soul, and these stormy agitations, and, by meditation on the precious promises of God, keep and establish your hearts.

Truly these times allow not the wonted security and the wonted intoxication of the world, but they demand that with honest groans we should cry for help, as the Lord saith, "Watch and pray that ye fall not into temptation," that ye may not, being overcome by despair, plunge into everlasting destruction. There is need of wisdom to discern the dangers of the soul, as well as the safeguard against them. Souls go to ruin as well when, in epicurean security, they make light of the wrath of God as when they are overcome by doubt and cast down by anxious sorrow, and these transgressions aggravate the punishment. The godly, on the other hand, who by faith and devotion keep their hearts erect and near to God, enjoy the beginning of eternal life and obtain mitigation of the general distress.

We, therefore, implore Thee, Son of God, Lord Jesus Christ, who, having been crucified and raised for us, standest in the secret counsel of the Godhead, and makest intercession for us, and hast said: "Come unto me, all ye that labor and are heavy laden, and I will give you rest." I call upon Thee, and with my whole heart beseech Thee, according to Thine infinite compassion, forgive us our sins. Thou knowest that in our great weakness we are not able to bear the burden of our wo. Do Thou, therefore, afford us aid in our private and public necessities; be Thou our shelter and protector, uphold the churches in these lands, and all which serves for their defense and safeguard.

KNOX

THE FIRST TEMPTATION OF CHRIST

BIOGRAPHICAL NOTE

JOHN KNOX, the great Scottish reformer, was born at Giffordgate, four miles from Haddington, Scotland, in 1505. He first made his appearance as a preacher in Edinburgh, where he thundered against popery, but was imprisoned and sent to the galleys in 1546. In 1547 Edward VI secured his release and made him a royal chaplain, when he acquired the friendship of Cranmer and other reformers. On the accession of Mary (1553) he took refuge on the Continent. In 1556 he accepted the charge of a church in Geneva, but, after three years of tranquillity, returned to Scotland and became a popular leader of the Reformation in that country. His eloquence lashed the multitude to enthusiasm and acts of turbulent violence. As a preacher his style was direct and fearless, often fiery, and he had a habit of pounding the pulpit to emphasize particular truths. He died in 1572.

KNOX
1505—1572

THE FIRST TEMPTATION OF CHRIST

Then was Jesus led up of the Spirit into the wilderness, to be tempted of the devil.—Matt. iv., 1.

THE cause moving me to treat of this place of Scripture is, that such as by the inscrutable providence of God fall into divers temptations, judge not themselves by reason thereof to be less acceptable in God's presence. But, on the contrary, having the way prepared to victory by Jesus Christ, they shall not fear above measure the crafty assaults of that subtle serpent Satan; but with joy and bold courage, having such a guide as here is pointed forth, such a champion, and such weapons as here are to be found (if with obedience we will hear, and unfeigned faith believe), we may assure ourselves of God's present favor, and of final victory, by the means of Him, who, for our safeguard and deliverance, entered in the battle, and triumphed over His adversary, and all his raging fury. And that this being heard and understood, may the better be kept in memory; this order, by God's grace, we propose to observe, in treating the matter: First, What this word temptation meaneth, and how it is used within the Scriptures. Secondly, Who is here tempted and at what time this temptation happened. Thirdly, How and by what means He was tempted. Fourthly, Why He should suffer these temptations, and what fruits ensue to us from the same.

First, Temptation, or to tempt, in the Scriptures of God, is called to try, to prove, or to assault the valor, the power, the will, the pleasure, or the wisdom—whether it be of God, or of creatures. And it is taken sometimes in good part, as when it is said that God tempted Abraham; God tempted the people of Israel; that is, God did try and examine them, not for His own knowledge, to whom nothing is hid, but to certify others how obedient Abraham was to God's commandment, and how weak and inferior Israelites were in their journey toward the promised land. And this temptation is always good, because it proceeds immediately from God, to open and make manifest the secret motions of men's hearts, the puissance and power of God's word, and the great lenity and gentleness of God toward the iniquities (yea, horrible sins and rebellions) of those whom He hath received into His regimen and care. For who could have believed that the bare word of God could so have moved the heart and affections of Abraham, that to obey God's commandment he determined to kill, with his own hand, his best-beloved son Isaac? Who could have trusted that, so many torments as Job suffered, he should not speak in all his great temptation one foolish word against God? Or who could have thought that God so mercifully should have pardoned so many and so manifest transgressions committed by His people in the desert, and yet that His mercy never utterly left them, but still continued with them, till at length he performed His promise made to Abraham? Who, I say, would have been persuaded of these things, unless by trials and temptations taken of His creatures by God, they had come by revelation made in His holy Scriptures to our knowledge? And so this kind of temptation is profitable, good, and necessary, as a thing proceeding from God, who is the fountain of all goodness, to the manifestation of His own glory, and to the profit of the suffered, however the flesh may judge in the hour of temptation. Otherwise temptation, or to tempt, is taken in evil part; that is, he that assaults or assails intends destruction and confusion to him that is assaulted. As when Satan tempted the women in the garden, Job by divers tribulations, and David by adultery. The scribes and Pharisees tempted Christ by divers means, questions, and subtleties. And of this matter, saith St. James, "God tempteth no man"; that is, by temptation proceeding immediately from Him He intends no man's destruction. And here you shall note, that altho Satan appears sometimes to prevail against God's elect, yet he is ever frustrated of his final purpose. By temptation He led Eve and David from the obedience of God, but He could not retain them forever under His thraldom. Power was granted to Him to spoil Job of his substance and children, and to strike his body with a plague and sickness most vile and fearful, but He could not compel his mouth to blaspheme God's majesty; and, therefore, altho we are laid open sometimes, as it were, to tribulation for a time, it is that when He has poured forth the venom of His malice against God's elect it may return to His own confusion, and that the deliverance of God's children may be more to His glory, and the comfort of the afflicted: knowing that His hand is so powerful, His mercy and good-will so prompt, that He delivers His little ones from their cruel enemy, even as David did his sheep and lambs from the mouth of the lion. For a little benefit received in extreme danger more moves us than the preservation from ten thousand perils, so that we fall not into them. And yet to preserve from dangers and perils so that we fall not into them, whether they are of body or spirit, is no less the work of God than to deliver from them; but the weakness of our faith does not perceive it: this I leave at the present.

Also, to tempt means simply to prove or try without any determinate purpose or profit or damage to ensue; as when the mind doubteth of anything, and therein desires to be satisfied, without great love or extreme hatred of the thing that is tempted or tried. David tempted; that is, tried himself if he could go in harness. (I Sam. xvii.) And Gideon said, "Let not thine anger kindle against me, if I tempt thee once again." So the Queen of Sheba came to tempt Solomon in subtle questions. This famous queen, not fully trusting the report and fame that was spread of Solomon, by subtle questions desired to prove his wisdom; at the first, neither extremely hating nor fervently loving the person of the king. And David, as a man not accustomed to harness, would try how he was able to go, and behave and fashion himself therein, before he would hazard battle with Goliath so armed. And Gideon, not satisfied in his conscience by the first that he received, desired, without contempt or hatred of God, a second time to be certified of his vocation. In this sense must the apostle be expounded when he commands us to tempt; that is, to try and examine ourselves, if we stand in the faith. Thus much for the term.

Now to the person tempted, and to the time and place of his temptation. The person tempted is the only well-beloved Son of God; the time was immediately after His baptism; and the place was the desert or wilderness. But that we derive advantage from what is related, we must consider the same more profoundly. That the Son of God was thus tempted gives instructions to us, that temptations, altho they be ever so grievous and fearful, do not separate us from God's favor and mercy, but rather declare the great graces of God to appertain to us, which makes Satan to rage as a roaring lion; for against none does He so fiercely fight as against those of whose hearts Christ has taken possession.

The time of Christ's temptation is here most diligently to be noted. And that was, as Mark and Luke witness, immediately after the voice of God the Father had commended His Son to the world, and had visibly pointed to Him by the sign of the Holy Ghost; He was led or moved by the Spirit to go to a wilderness, where forty days he remained fasting among the wild beasts. This Spirit which led Christ into the wilderness was not the devil, but the holy Spirit of God the Father, by whom Christ, as touching His human and manly nature, was conducted and led; likewise by the same Spirit He was strengthened and made strong, and, finally, raised up from the dead. The Spirit of God, I say, led Christ to the place of His battle, where He endured the combat for the whole forty days and nights. As Luke saith, "He was tempted," but in the end most vehemently, after His continual fasting, and that He began to be hungry. Upon this forty days and this fasting of Christ do our Papists found and build their Lent; for, say they, all the actions of Christ are our instructions; what He did we ought to follow. But He fasted forty days, therefore we ought to do the like. I answer, that if we ought to follow all Christ's actions, then ought we neither to eat nor drink for the space of forty days, for so fasted Christ; we ought to go upon the waters with our feet; to cast out devils by our word; to heal and cure all sorts of maladies; to call again the dead to life; for so did Christ. This I write only that men may see the vanity of those who, boasting themselves of wisdom, have become fools.

Did Christ fast those forty days to teach us superstitious fasting? Can the Papists assure me, or any other man, which were the forty days that Christ fasted? plain it is he fasted the forty days and nights that immediately followed His baptism, but which they were, or in what month was the day of His baptism, Scripture does not express; and altho the day were exprest, am I or any Christian bound to counterfeit Christ's actions as the ape counterfeits the act or work of man? He Himself requires no such obedience of His true followers, but saith to the apostles, "Go and preach the gospel to all nations, baptizing them in the name of the Father, the Son, and the Holy Ghost; commanding them to observe and keep all that I have commanded you." Here Christ Jesus requires the observance of His precepts and commandments, not of His actions, except in so far as He had also commanded them; and so must the apostle be understood when he saith, "Be followers of Christ, for Christ hath suffered for us, that we should follow His footsteps," which can not be understood of every action of Christ, either in the mystery of our redemption, or in His actions and marvelous works, but only of those which He hath commanded us to observe. But where the Papists are so diligent in establishing their dreams and fantasies, they lose the profit that here is to be gathered; that is, why Christ fasted those forty days; which were a doctrine more necessary for Christians than to corrupt the simple hearts with superstition, as tho the wisdom of God, Christ Jesus, had taught us no other mystery by His fasting than the abstinence from flesh, or once on the day to eat flesh, for the space of forty days. God hath taken a just vengeance upon the pride of such men, while He thus confounds the wisdom of those that do most glory in wisdom, and strikes with blindness such as will be guides and lanterns to the feet of others, and yet refuse themselves to hear or follow the light of God's word. From such deliver thy poor flock, O Lord!

The uses of Christ's fasting these forty days I find chiefly to be two: The first, to witness to the world the dignity and excellence of His vocation, which Christ, after His baptism, was to take upon Him openly; the other, to declare that he entered into battle willingly for our cause, and does, as it were, provoke his adversary to assault Him: altho Christ Jesus, in the eternal counsel of His Father, was appointed to be the Prince of Peace, the angel (that is, the messenger) of His testament, and He alone that could fight our battles for us, yet He did not enter in execution of it, in the sight of men, till He was commended to mankind by the voice of His heavenly Father; and as He was placed and anointed by the Holy Ghost by a visible sign given to the eyes of men. After which time He was led to the desert, and fasted, as before is said; and this He did to teach us with what fear, carefulness, and reverence the messengers of the Word ought to enter on their vocation, which is not only most excellent (for who is worthy to be God's ambassador?) but also subject to most extreme troubles and dangers. For he that is appointed pastor, watchman, or preacher, if he feed not with his whole power, if he warn and admonish not when he sees the snare come, and if, in doctrine, he divide not the Word righteously, the blood and souls of those that perish for lack of food, admonition, and doctrine shall be required of his hand.

But to our purpose; that Christ exceeded not the space of forty days in His fasting, He did it to the imitation of Moses and Elias; of whom, the one before the receiving of the law, and the other before the communication and reasoning which he had with God in Mount Horeb, in which He was commanded to anoint Hazael king over Syria, and Jehu king over Israel, and Elisha to be prophet, fasted the same number of days. The events that ensued and followed this supernatural fasting of these two servants of God, Moses and Elias, impaired and diminished the tyranny of the kingdom of Satan. For by the law came the knowledge of sin, the damnation of such impieties, specially of idolatry, and such as the devil had invented; and, finally, by the law came such a revelation of God's will that no man could justly afterward excuse his sin by ignorance, by which the devil before had blinded many. So that the law, altho it might not renew and purge the heart, for that the Spirit of Christ Jesus worketh by faith only, yet it was a bridle that did hinder and stay the rage of external wickedness in many, and was a schoolmaster that led unto Christ. For when man can find no power in himself to do that which is commanded, and perfectly understands, and when he believes that the curse of God is pronounced against those that abide not in everything that is commanded in God's law to do them—the man, I say, that understands and knows his own corrupt nature and God's severe judgment, most gladly will receive the free redemption offered by Christ Jesus, which is the only victory that overthrows Satan and his power. And so by the giving of the law God greatly weakened, impaired, and made frail the tyranny and kingdom of the devil. In the days of Elias, the devil had so prevailed that kings and rulers made open war against God, killing His prophets, destroying His ordinances, and building up idolatry, which did so prevail that the prophet complained that of all the true fearers and worshipers of God he was left alone, and wicked Jezebel sought His life also. After this, his fasting and complaint, he was sent by God to anoint the persons aforenamed, who took such vengeance upon the wicked and obstinate idolaters that he who escaped the sword of Hazael fell into the hands of Jehu, and those whom Jehu left escaped not God's vengeance under Elisha.

The remembrance of this was fearful to Satan, for, at the coming of Christ Jesus, impiety was in the highest degree among those that pretended most knowledge of God's will; and Satan was at such rest in his kingdom that the priests, scribes and Pharisees had taken away the key of knowledge; that is, they had so obscured and darkened God's

Holy Scriptures, by false glosses and vain traditions, that neither would they themselves enter into the kingdom of God, nor suffer and permit others to enter; but with violence restrained, and with tyranny struck back from the right way, that is, from Christ Jesus Himself, such as would have entered into the possession of life everlasting by Him. Satan, I say, having such dominion over the chief rulers of the visible Church, and espying in Christ, such graces as before he had not seen in man, and considering Him to follow in fasting the footsteps of Moses and Elias, no doubt greatly feared that the quietness and rest of his most obedient servants, the priests, and their adherents, would be troubled by Christ. And, therefore, by all engines and craft, he assaults Him to see what advantage he could have of Him. And Christ did not repel him, as by the power of His Godhead He might have done, that he should not tempt Him, but permitted him to spend all his artillery, and received the strokes and assaults of Satan's temptations in His own body, to the end He might weaken and enfeeble the strength and tyrannous power of our adversary by His long suffering. For thus, methinks, our Master and Champion, Jesus Christ, provoked our enemy to battle: "Satan, thou gloriest of thy power and victories over mankind, that there is none able to withstand thy assaults, nor escape thy darts, but at one time or other thou givest him a wound: lo! I am a man like to my brethren, having flesh and blood, and all properties of man's nature (sin, which is thy venom, excepted); tempt, try, and assault me; I offer you here a place most convenient—the wilderness. There shall be no mortal to comfort me against thy assaults; thou shalt have time sufficient; do what thou canst, I shall not fly the place of battle. If thou become victor, thou shalt still continue in possession of thy kingdom in this wretched world; but if thou canst not prevail against me, then must thy prey and unjust spoil be taken from thee; thou must grant thyself vanquished and confounded, and must be compelled to leave off from all accusation of the members of my body; for to them appertains the fruit of my battle, my victory is theirs, as I am appointed to take the punishment of their sins in my body."

What comfort ought the remembrance of these signs to be to our hearts! Christ Jesus hath fought our battle; He Himself hath taken us into His care and protection; however the devil may rage by temptations, be they spiritual or corporeal, he is not able to bereave us out of the hand of the almighty Son of God. To Him be all glory for His mercies most abundantly poured upon us!

There remains yet to be spoken of the time when our Lord was tempted, which began immediately after His baptism. Whereupon we have to note the mark, that altho the malice of Satan never ceases, but always seeks for means to trouble the godly, yet sometimes he rages more fiercely than others, and that is commonly when God begins to manifest His love and favor to any of His children, and at the end of their battle, when they are nearest to obtain final victory. The devil, no doubt, did at all times envy the humble spirit that was in Abel, but he did not stir up the cruel heart of Cain against him till God declared His favor toward him by accepting his sacrifice. The same we find in Jacob, Joseph, David, and most evidently in Christ Jesus. How Satan raged at the tidings of Christ's nativity! what blood he caused to be shed on purpose to have murdered Christ in His infancy! The evangelist St. Matthew witnesses that in all the coasts and borders of Bethlehem the children of two years old and less age were murdered without mercy. A fearful spectacle and horrid example of insolent and unaccustomed tyranny! And what is the cause moving Satan thus to rage against innocents, considering that by reason of their imperfections they could not hurt his kingdom at that instant? Oh, the crafty eye of Satan looked farther than to the present time; he heard reports by the three wise men, that they had learned by the appearance of a star that the King of the Jews was born;

and he was not ignorant that the time prophesied of Christ's coming was then instant; for a stranger was clad with the crown and scepter of Judah. The angel had declared the glad tidings to the shepherds, that a Savior, which was Christ the Lord, was born in the city of David. All these tidings inflamed the wrath and malice of Satan, for he perfectly understood that the coming of the promised Seed was appointed to his confusion, and to the breaking down of his head and tyranny; and therefore he raged most cruelly, even at the first hearing of Christ's birth, thinking that altho he could not hinder nor withstand His coming, yet he could shorten his days upon earth, lest by long life and peaceable quietness in it, the number of good men, by Christ's doctrine and virtuous life, should be multiplied; and so he strove to cut Him away among the other children before He could open His mouth on His Father's message. Oh, cruel serpent! in vain dost thou spend thy venom, for the days of God's elect thou canst not shorten! And when the wheat is fallen on the ground, then doth it most multiply.

But from these things mark, what hath been the practise of the devil from the beginning—most cruelly to rage against God's children when God begins to show them His mercy. And, therefore, marvel not, dearly beloved, altho the like come unto you.

If Satan fume or roar against you, whether it be against your bodies by persecution, or inwardly in your conscience by a spiritual battle, be not discouraged, as tho you were less acceptable in God's presence, or as if Satan might at any time prevail against you. No; your temptations and storms, that arise so suddenly, argue and witness that the seed which is sown is fallen on good ground, begins to take root and shall, by God's grace, bring forth fruit abundantly in due season and convenient time. That is it which Satan fears, and therefore thus he rages, and shall rage against you, thinking that if he can repulse you now suddenly in the beginning, that then you shall be at all times an easy prey, never able to resist his assaults. But as my hope is good, so shall my prayer be, that so you may be strengthened, that the world and Satan himself may perceive or understand that God fights your battle. For you remember that being present with you and treating of the same place, I admonished you that Satan could not long sleep when his kingdom was threatened. And therefore I willed you, if you were in mind to continue with Christ, to prepare yourselves for the day of temptation. The person of the speaker is wretched, miserable, and nothing to be regarded, but the things that were spoken are the infallible and eternal truth of God; without observation of which, life neither can or shall come to mankind. God grant you continuance to the end.

This much have I briefly spoken of the temptation of Christ Jesus, who was tempted; and of the time and place of His temptation. Now remains to be spoken how He was tempted, and by what means. The most part of expositors think that all this temptation was in spirit and in imagination only, the corporeal senses being nothing moved. I will contend with no man in such cases, but patiently will I suffer every man to abound in his own knowledge; and without prejudice of any man's estimation, I offer my judgment to be weighed and considered by Christian charity. It appears to me by the plain text that Christ suffered this temptation in body and spirit. Likewise, as the hunger which Christ suffered, and the desert in which He remained, were not things offered to the imagination, but that the body did verily remain in the wilderness among beasts, and after forty days did hunger and faint for lack of food; so the external ear did hear the tempting words of Satan, which entered into the knowledge of the soul, and which, repelling the venom of such temptations, caused the tongue to speak and confute Satan, to our unspeakable comfort and consolation. It appears also that the body of Christ Jesus was carried by Satan from the wilderness unto the temple of Jerusalem, and that it was placed upon the pinnacle of the same temple, from whence it was carried to a high mountain and there tempted. If any man can show to the contrary hereof by the plain Scriptures of God, with all submission and thanksgiving I will prefer his judgment to my own; but if the matter stand only in probability and opinion of men, then it is lawful for me to believe as the Scripture here speaks; that is, that Satan spake and Christ answered, and Satan took Him and carried Him from one place to another. Besides the evidence of the text affirming that Satan was permitted to carry the body of Christ from place to place, and yet was not permitted to execute any further tyranny against it, is most singular comfort to such as are afflicted or troubled in body or spirit. The weak and feeble conscience of man under such temptations, commonly gathers and collects a false consequence. For man reasons thus: The body or the spirit is vexed by assaults and temptations of Satan, and he troubles or molests it, therefore God is angry with it, and takes no care of it. I answer, tribulations or grievous vexations of body or of mind are never signs of God's displeasure against the sufferer, neither yet does it follow that God has cast away the care of His creatures because He permits them to be molested and vexed for a time. For if any sort of tribulation were the infallible sign of God's displeasure, then should we condemn the best beloved children of God. But of this we may speak hereafter. Now to the temptation.

Verse 2. "And when he fasteth forty days and forty nights, He was afterwards an hungered." Verse 3. 'Then came to Him the tempter,' and said, 'If you be the Son of God, command that these stones be made bread," etc. Why Christ fasted forty days and would not exceed the same, without sense and feeling of hunger, is before touched upon, that is, He would provoke the devil to battle by the wilderness and long abstinence, but He would not usurp or arrogate any more to Himself in that case than God had wrought with others, His servants and messengers before. But Christ Jesus (as St. Augustine more amply declares), without feeling of hunger, might have endured the whole year, or to time without end, as well as He did endure the space of forty days. For the nature of mankind was sustained those forty days by the invisible power of God, which is at all times of equal power. But Christ, willing to offer further occasion to Satan to proceed in tempting of Him, permitted the human nature to crave earnestly that which it lacked, that is to say, refreshing of meat; which Satan perceiving took occasion, as before, to tempt and assault. Some judge that Satan tempted Christ to gluttony, but this appears little to agree with the purpose of the Holy

Ghost; who shows us this history to let us understand that Satan never ceases to oppugn the children of God, but continually, by one mean or other, drives or provokes them to some wicked opinions of their God; and to have them desire stones to be converted into bread, or to desire hunger to be satisfied, has never been sin, nor yet a wicked opinion of God. And therefore I doubt not but the temptation was more spiritual, more subtle, and more dangerous. Satan had respect to the voice of God, which had pronounced Christ to be His well-beloved Son, etc. Against this voice he fights, as his nature is ever to do against the assured and immutable Word of God; for such is his malice against God, and against His chosen children, that where and to whom God pronounces love and mercy, to these he threatens displeasures and damnation; and where God threatens death, there is he bold to pronounce life; and for this course is Satan called a liar from the beginning. And so the purpose of Satan was to drive Christ into desperation, that he should not believe the former voice of God His Father; which appears to be the meaning of this temptation: "Thou hast heard," would Satan say, "a voice proclaimed in the air, that Thou wast the beloved Son of God, in whom His soul was pleased; but mayst Thou not be judged more than mad, and weaker than the brainless fool if Thou believest any such promise? Where are the signs of His love? Art Thou not cast out from comfort of all creatures? Thou art in worse case than the brute beasts, for every day they hunt for their prey, and the earth produces grass and herbs for their sustenance, so that none of them are pined and consumed away by hunger; but Thou hast fasted forty days and nights, ever waiting for some relief and comfort from above, but Thy best provision is hard stones! If Thou dost glory in thy God, and dost verily believe the promise that is made, command that these stones be bread. But evident it is that so Thou canst not do; for if Thou couldst, or if Thy God would have showed Thee any such pleasure, Thou mightest long ago have removed Thy hunger, and needest not have endured this languishing for lack of food. But seeing Thou hast long continued thus, and no provision is made for Thee, it is vanity longer to believe any such promise, and therefore despair of any help from God's hand, and provide for Thyself by some other means!"

Many words have I used here, dearly beloved, but I can not express the thousandth part of the malicious despite which lurked in this one temptation of Satan. It was a mocking of Christ and of His obedience. It was a plain denial of God's promise. It was the triumphing voice of him that appeared to have gotten victory. Oh, how bitter this temptation was no creature can understand but such as feel the grief of such darts as Satan casts at the tender conscience of those that gladly would rest and repose in God, and in the promises of His mercy. But here is to be noted the ground and foundation. The conclusion of Satan is this: Thou art none of God's elect, much less His well-beloved Son. His reason is this: Thou art in trouble and findest no relief. There the foundation of the temptation was Christ's poverty, and the lack of food without hope of remedy to be sent from God. And it is the same temptation which the devil objected to Him by the princes of the priests in His grievous torments upon the cross; for thus they cried, "If he be the Son of God, let him come down from the cross and we will believe in him; he trusted in God, let him deliver him, if he have the pleasure in him." As tho they would say, God is the deliverer of His servants from troubles; God never permits those that fear Him to come to confusion; this man we see in extreme trouble; if He be the Son of God, or even a true worshiper of His name, He will deliver Him from this calamity. If He deliver Him not, but suffer Him to perish in these anguishes, then it is an assured sign that God has rejected Him as a hypocrite, that shall have no portion of His glory. Thus, I say, Satan takes occasion to tempt, and moves also others to judge and condemn God's elect and chosen children, by reason that troubles are multiplied upon them.

But with what weapons we ought to fight against such enemies and assaults we shall learn in the answer of Christ Jesus, which follows: But He, answering, said "It is written, man shall not live by bread alone, but by every word which proceedeth out of the mouth of God." This answer of Christ proves the sentence which we have brought of the aforesaid temptation to be the very meaning of the Holy Ghost; for unless the purpose of Satan has been to have removed Christ from all hope of God's merciful providence toward Him in that His necessity, Christ had not answered directly to his words, saying, "Command that these stones be made bread." But Christ Jesus, perceiving his art and malicious subtilty, answered directly to his meaning, His words nothing regarded; by which Satan was so confounded that he was ashamed to reply any further.

But that you may the better understand the meaning of Christ's answer, we will express and repeat it over in more words. "Thou laborest, Satan," would Christ say, "to bring into my heart a doubt and suspicion of My Father's promise, which was openly proclaimed in My baptism, by reason of My hunger, and that I lack all carnal provision. Thou art bold to affirm that God takes no care for Me, but thou art a deceitful and false corrupt sophister, and thy argument, too, is vain, and full of blasphemies; for thou bindest God's love, mercy, and providence to the having or wanting of bodily provision, which no part of God's Scriptures teach us, but rather the express contrary. As it is written, 'Man doth not live by bread alone, but by every word that proceedeth out of the mouth of God,' that is, the very life and felicity of man consists not in the abundance of bodily things, or the possession and having of them makes no man blest or happy; neither shall the lack of them be the cause of his final misery; but the very life of man consists in God, and in His promises pronounced by His own mouth, unto which whoso cleaves unfeignedly shall live the life everlasting. And altho all creatures in earth forsake him, yet shall not his bodily life perish till the time appointed by God approach. For God has means to feed, preserve, and maintain, unknown to man's reason, and contrary to the common course of nature. He fed His people Israel in the desert forty years without the provision of man. He preserved Jonah in the whale's belly; and maintained and kept the bodies of the three children in the furnace of fire. Reason and the natural man could have seen nothing in these cases but destruction and death, and could have judged nothing but that God had cast away the care of these, His creatures, and yet His providence was most vigilant toward them in the extremity of their dangers, from which He did so deliver them, and in the midst of them did so assist them, that His glory, which is His mercy and goodness, did more appear and shine after their troubles than it could have done if they had fallen in them. And therefore I measure not the truth and favor of God by having or by lacking of bodily necessities, but by the promise which He has made to me. As He Himself is immutable, so is His word and promise constant, which I believe, and to which I will adhere, and so cleave, whatever can come to the body outwardly.''

In this answer of Christ we may perceive what weapons are to be used against our adversary the devil, and how we may confute his arguments, which craftily, and of malice, he makes against God's elect. Christ might have repulsed Satan with a word, or by commanding him to silence, as He to whom all power was given in heaven and earth; but it pleased His mercy to teach us how to use the sword of the Holy Ghost, which is the word of God, in battle against our spiritual enemy. The Scripture which Christ brings is written in the eighth chapter of Deuteronomy. It was spoken by Moses a little before His death, to establish the people in God's merciful providence. For in the same chapter, and in certain others that go before, He reckons the great travail and divers dangers with the extreme necessities that they had sustained in the desert the space of forty years, and yet, notwithstanding how constant God had been in keeping and performing His promise, for throughout all perils He had conducted them to the sight and borders of the promised land. And so this Scripture more directly answers to the temptation of Satan; for thus does Satan reason, as before is said, "Thou art in poverty and hast no provision to sustain thy life. Therefore God takes no regard nor care of Thee, as He doth over His chosen children." Christ Jesus answered: "Thy argument is false and vain; for poverty or necessity precludes not the providence or care of God; which is easy to be proved by the people of God, Israel, who, in the desert, oftentimes lacked things necessary to the sustenance of life, and for lack of the same they grudged and murmured; yet the Lord never cast away the providence and care of them, but according to the word that He had once pronounced, to wit, that they were His peculiar people; and according to the promise made to Abraham, and to them before their departure from Egypt, He still remained their conductor and guide, till He placed them in peaceable possession of the land of Canaan, their great infirmities and manifold transgressions notwithstanding."

Thus are we taught, I say, by Christ Jesus, to repulse Satan and his assaults by the Word of God, and to apply the examples of His mercies, which He has shown to others before us, to our own souls in the hour of temptation, and in the time of our trouble. For what God doth to one at any time, the same appertains to all that depend upon God and His promises. And, therefore, however we are assaulted by Satan, our adversary, within the Word of God is armor and weapons sufficient. The chief craft of Satan is to trouble those that begin to decline from his obedience, and to declare themselves enemies to iniquity, with divers assaults, the design whereof is always the same; that is, to put variance betwixt them and God into their conscience, that they should not repose and rest themselves in His assured promises. And to persuade this, he uses and invents divers arguments. Sometimes he calls the sins of their youth, and which they have committed in the time of blindness, to their remembrance; very often he objects their unthankfulness toward God and present imperfections. By sickness, poverty, tribulations in their household, or by persecution, he can allege that God is angry, and regard them not. Or by the spiritual cross which few feel and fewer understand the utility and profit of, he would drive God's children to desperation, and by infinite means more, he goeth about seeking, like a roaring lion, to undermine and destroy our faith. But it is imposible for him to prevail against us unless we obstinately refuse to use the defense and weapons that God has offered. Yea, I say, that God's elect can not refuse it, but seek for their Defender when the battle is most strong; for the sobs, groans, and lamentations of such as fight, yea, the fear they have lest they be vanquished, the calling and prayer for continuance, are the undoubted and right seeking of Christ our champion. We refuse not the weapon, altho sometimes, by infirmity, we can not use it as we would. It suffices that your hearts unfeignedly sob for greater strength, for continuance, and for final deliverance by Christ Jesus; that which is wanting in us, His sufficiency doth supply; for it is He that fighteth and overcometh for us. But for bringing of the examples of the Scriptures, if God permit, in the end we shall speak more largely when it shall be treated why Christ permitted Himself thus to be tempted. Sundry impediments now call me from writing in this matter, but, by God's grace, at convenient leisure I purpose to finish, and to send it to you. I grant the matter that proceeds from me is not worthy of your pain and labor to read it; yet, seeing it is a testimony of my good mind toward you, I doubt not but you will accept it in good part. God, the Father of our Lord Jesus Christ, grant unto you to find favor and mercy of the Judge, whose eyes and knowledge pierce through the secret cogitations of the heart, in the day of temptation, which shall come upon all flesh, according to that mercy which you (illuminated and directed by His Holy Spirit) have showed to the afflicted. Now the God of all comfort and consolation confirm and strengthen you in His power unto the end. Amen.

CALVIN

ENDURING PERSECUTION FOR CHRIST

BIOGRAPHICAL NOTE

JOHN CALVIN was born in 1509, at Noyon, France. He has been called the greatest of Protestant commentators and theologians, and the inspirer of the Puritan exodus. He often preached every day for weeks in succession. He possest two of the greatest elements in successful pulpit oratory, self-reliance and authority. It was said of him, as it was afterward said of Webster, that "every word weighed a pound." His style was simple, direct, and convincing. He made men think. His splendid contributions to religious thought, and his influence upon individual liberty, give him a distinguished place among great reformers and preachers. His idea of preaching is thus exprest in his own words: "True preaching must not be dead, but living and effective. No parade of rhetoric, but the Spirit of God must resound in the voice in order to operate with power." He died at Geneva in 1564.

CALVIN
1509—1564

ENDURING PERSECUTION FOR CHRIST

Let us go forth therefore unto him without the camp bearing his reproach.—Hebrews xiii., 13.

ALL the exhortations which can be given us to suffer patiently for the name of Jesus Christ, and in defense of the gospel, will have no effect if we do not feel assured of the cause for which we fight. For when we are called to part with life, it is absolutely necessary to know on what grounds. The firmness necessary we can not possess, unless it be founded on certainty of faith.

It is true that persons may be found who will foolishly expose themselves to death in maintaining some absurd opinions and dreams conceived by their own brain, but such impetuosity is more to be regarded as frenzy than as Christian zeal; and, in fact, there is neither firmness nor sound sense in those who thus, at a kind of haphazard, cast themselves away. But, however this may be, it is in a good cause only that God can acknowledge us as His martyrs. Death is common to all, and the children of God are condemned to ignominy and tortures as criminals are; but God makes the distinction between them, inasmuch as He can not deny His truth. On our part, then, it is requisite that we have sure and infallible evidence of the doctrine which we maintain; and hence, as I have said, we can not be rationally imprest by any exhortations which we receive to suffer persecution for the gospel, if no true certainty of faith has been imprinted in our hearts. For to hazard our life upon a peradventure is not natural, and tho we were to do it, it would only be rashness, not Christian courage. In a word, nothing that we do will be approved of God if we are not thoroughly persuaded that it is for Him and His cause we suffer persecution, and the world is our enemy.

Now, when I speak of such persuasion, I mean not merely that we must know how to distinguish between true religion and the abuses or follies of men, but also that we must be thoroughly persuaded of the heavenly life, and the crown which is promised us above, after we shall have fought here below. Let us understand, then, that both of these requisites are necessary, and can not be separated from each other. The points, accordingly, with which we must commence are these: We must know well what our Christianity is, what the faith which we have to hold and follow, what the rule which God has given us; and we must be so well furnished with such instructions as to be able boldly to condemn all the falsehoods, errors, and superstitions which Satan has introduced to corrupt the pure simplicity of the doctrine of God. Hence, we ought not to be surprized that, in the present day, we see so few persons disposed to suffer for the gospel, and that the greater part of those who call themselves Christians know not what it is. For all are, as it were, lukewarm; and instead of making it their business to hear or read, count it enough to have had some slight taste of Christian faith. This is the reason why there is so little decision, and why those who are assailed immediately fall away. This fact should stimulate us to inquire more diligently into divine truth, in order to be well assured with regard to it.

Still, however, to be well informed and grounded is not the whole that is necessary. For we see some who seem to be thoroughly imbued with sound doctrine, and who, notwithstanding, have no more zeal or affection than if they had never known any more of God than some fleeting fancy. Why is this? Just because they have never comprehended the majesty of the Holy Scriptures. And, in fact, did we, such as we are, consider well that it is God who speaks to us, it is certain that we would listen more attentively, and with greater reverence. If we would think that in reading Scripture we are in the school of angels, we would be far more careful and desirous to profit by the doctrine which is propounded to us.

We now see the true method of preparing to suffer for the gospel. First, We must have profited so far in the school of God as to be decided in regard to true religion and the doctrine which we are to hold; and we must despise all the wiles and impostures of Satan, and all human inventions, as things not only frivolous but also carnal, inasmuch as they corrupt Christian purity; therein differing, like true martyrs of Christ, from the fantastic persons who suffer for mere absurdities. Second, Feeling assured of the good cause, we must be inflamed, accordingly, to follow God whithersoever He may call us: His Word must have such authority with us as it deserves, and having withdrawn from this world, we must feel as it were enraptured in seeking the heavenly life.

But it is more than strange that, tho the light of God is shining more brightly than it ever did before, there is a lamentable want of zeal! If the thought does not fill us with shame, so much the worse. For we must shortly come before the great Judge, where the iniquity which we endeavor to hide will be brought forward with such upbraidings that we shall be utterly confounded. For, if we are obliged to bear testimony to God, according to the measure of the knowledge which He has given us, to what is it owing, I would ask, that we are so cold and timorous in entering into battle, seeing that God has so fully manifested Himself at this time that He may be said to have opened to us and displayed before us the great treasures of His secrets? May it not be said that we do not think we have to do with God? For had we any regard to His Majesty we would not dare to turn the doctrine which proceeds from Him into some kind of philosophic speculation. In short, it is impossible to deny that it is our great shame, not to say fearful condemnation, that we have so well known the truth of God, and have so little courage to maintain it!

Above all, when we look to the martyrs of past times, well may we detest our own cowardice! The greater part of those were not persons much versed in Holy Scripture, so as to be able to dispute on all subjects. They knew that there was one God, whom they behooved to worship and serve—that they had been redeemed by the blood of Jesus Christ, in order that they might place their confidence of salvation in Him and in His grace—and that, all the inventions of men being mere dross and rubbish, they ought to condemn all idolatries and superstitions. In one word, their theology was in substance this—There is one God who created all the world, and declared His will to us by Moses and the prophets, and finally by Jesus Christ and His apostles; and we have one sole Redeemer, who purchased us by His blood, and by whose grace we hope to be saved: All the idols of the world are curst, and deserve execration.

With a system embracing no other points than these, they went boldly to the flames, or to any other kind of death. They did not go in twos or threes, but in such bands that the number of those who fell by the hands of tyrants is almost infinite! We, on our part, are such learned clerks that none can be more so (so at least we think), and, in fact, so far as regards the knowledge of Scripture, God has so spread it out before us that no former age was ever so highly favored. Still, after all, there is scarcely a particle of zeal. When men manifest such indifference, it looks as if they were bent on provoking the vengeance of God.

What then should be done in order to inspire our breasts with true courage? We have, in the first place, to consider how precious the confession of our faith is in the sight of God. We little know how much God prizes it, if our life, which is nothing, is valued by us more highly. When it is so, we manifest a marvelous degree of stupidity. We can not save our life at the expense of our confession without acknowledging that we hold it in higher estimation than the honor of God and the salvation of our souls.

A heathen could say that "It was a miserable thing to save life by giving up the only things which made life desirable!" And yet he and others like him never knew for what end men are placed in the world, and why they live in it. It is true they knew enough to say that men ought to follow virtue, to conduct themselves honestly and without reproach; but all their virtues were mere paint and smoke. We know far better what the chief aim of life should be, namely, to glorify God, in order that He may be our glory. When this is not done, wo to us! And we can not continue to live for a single moment upon the earth without heaping additional curses on our heads. Still we are not ashamed to purchase some few days to languish here below, renouncing eternal kingdom by separating ourselves from Him by whose energy we are sustained in life.

Were we to ask the most ignorant, not to say the most brutish, persons in the world why they live, they would not venture to answer simply that it is to eat, and drink, and sleep; for all know that they have been created for a higher and holier end. And what end can we find if it be not to honor God, and allow ourselves to be governed by Him, like children by good parents; so that after we have finished the journey of this corruptible life, we may be received into His eternal inheritance? Such is the principal, indeed the sole end. When we do not take it into account, and are intent on a brutish life, which is worse than a thousand deaths, what can we allege for our excuse? To live and not know why is unnatural. To reject the causes for which we live, under the influence of a foolish longing for a respite of some few days, during which we are to live in the world, while separated from God—I know not how to name such infatuation and madness!

But as persecution is always harsh and bitter, let us consider how and by what means Christians may be able to fortify themselves with patience, so as unflinchingly to expose their life for the truth of God. The text which we have read out, when it is properly understood, is sufficient to induce us to do so. The apostle says, Let us go forth from the city after the Lord Jesus, bearing His reproach. In the first place, he reminds us, altho the swords should not be drawn against us nor the fires kindled to burn us, that we can not be truly united to the Son of God while we are rooted in this world. Wherefore a Christian, even in repose, must always have one foot lifted to march to battle, and not only so, but he must have his affections withdrawn from the world, altho his body is dwelling in it. Grant that this at first sight seems to us hard, still we must be satisfied with the words of St. Paul (I Thess. iii.), that we are called and appointed to suffer. As if He had said, Such is our condition as Christians; this is the road by which we must go if we would follow Christ.

Meanwhile, to solace our infirmity and mitigate the vexation and sorrow which persecution might cause us, a good reward is held forth: In suffering for the cause of God, we are walking step by step after the Son of God, and have Him for our guide. Were it simply said that to be Christians we must pass through all the insults of the world boldly, to meet death at all times and in whatever way God may be pleased to appoint, we might apparently have some pretext for replying that it is a strange road to go at peradventure. But when we are commanded to follow the Lord Jesus, His guidance is too good and honorable to be refused. Now, in order that we may be more deeply moved, not only is it said that Jesus Christ walks before us as our Captain, but that we are made conformable to His image; so St. Paul says in the eighth chapter to the Romans that God hath ordained all those whom He hath adopted for His children, to be made conformable to Him who is the pattern and head of all.

Are we so delicate as to be unwilling to endure anything? Then we must renounce the grace of God by which He has called us to the hope of salvation. For there are two things which can not be separated—to be members of Christ, and to be tried by many afflictions. We certainly ought to prize such a conformity to the Son of God much more than we do. It is true, that in the world's judgment there is disgrace in suffering for the gospel. But since we know that believers are blind, ought we not to have better eyes than they? It is ignominy to suffer from those who occupy the seat of justice, but St. Paul shows us by his example that we have to glory in scourings for Jesus Christ, as marks by which God recognizes us and avows us for His own. And we know what St. Luke narrates of Peter and John (Acts v., 41); namely, that they rejoiced to have been counted worthy to suffer infamy and reproach for the name of the Lord Jesus.

Ignominy and dignity are two opposites: so says the world, which, being infatuated, judges against all reason, and in this way converts the glory of God into dishonor. But, on our part, let us not refuse to be vilified as concerns the world, in order to be honored before God and His angels. We see what pains the ambitious take to receive the commands of a king, and what a boast they make of it. The Son of God presents His commands to us, and every one stands back. Tell me, pray, whether in so doing are we worthy of having anything in common with Him? there is nothing here to attract our sensual nature, but such notwithstanding are the true escutcheons of nobility in the heavens. Imprisonment, exile, evil report, imply in men's imagination whatever is to be vituperated; but what hinders us from viewing things as God judges and declares them, save our unbelief? Wherefore, let the name of the Son of God have all the weight with us which it deserves, that we may learn to count it honor when He stamps His marks upon us. If we act otherwise our ingratitude is insupportable.

Were God to deal with us according to our desserts, would He not have just cause to chastise us daily in a thousand ways? Nay more, a hundred thousand deaths would not suffice for a small portion of our misdeeds! Now, if in His infinite goodness He puts all our faults under His foot and abolishes them, and instead of punishing us according to our demerit, devises an admirable means to convert our afflictions into honor and a special privilege, inasmuch as through them we are taken into partnership with His Son, must it not be said, when we disdain such a happy state, that we have indeed made little progress in Christian doctrine?

Accordingly, St. Peter, after exhorting us (I Peter iv., 15) to walk so purely in the fear of God, as not to suffer as thieves, adulterers, and murderers, immediately adds, that if we must suffer as Christians, let us glorify God for the blessing which He thus bestows upon us. It is not without cause he speaks thus. For who are we, I pray, to be witnesses of the truth of God, and advocates to maintain His cause? Here we are poor worms of the earth, creatures full of vanity, full of lies, and yet God employs us to defend His truth—an honor which pertains not even to the angels of heaven! May not this consideration alone well inflame us to offer ourselves to God to be employed in any way in such honorable service?

Many persons, however, can not refrain from pleading against God, or, at least, from complaining against Him for not better supporting their weakness. It is marvelously strange, they say, how God, after having chosen us for His children, allows us to be trampled upon and tormented by the ungodly. I answer: Even were it not apparent why He does so, He might well exercise His authority over us, and fix our lot at His pleasure. But when we see that Jesus Christ is our pattern, ought we not, without inquiring further, to esteem it great happiness that we are made like Him? God, however, makes it very apparent what the reasons are for which He is pleased that we should be persecuted. Had we nothing more than the consideration suggested by St. Peter (I Peter i., 7), we were disdainful indeed not to acquiesce in it. He says that since gold and silver, which are only corruptible metals, are purified and tested by fire, it is but reasonable that our faith, which surpasses all the riches of the world, should be so tried.

It were easy indeed for God to crown us at once without requiring us to sustain any combats; but as it is His pleasure that until the end of the world Christ shall reign in the midst of His enemies, so it is also His pleasure that we, being placed in the midst of them, shall suffer their oppression and violence till He deliver us. I know, indeed, that the flesh rebels when it is to be brought to this point, but still the will of God must have the mastery. If we feel some repugnance in ourselves, it need not surprize us; for it is only too natural for us to shun the cross. Still let us not fail to surmount it, knowing that God accepts our obedience, provided we bring all our feelings and wishes into captivity, and make them subject to Him.

When prophets and apostles went to death, it was not without feeling some inclination to recoil. "They shall carry thee whither thou wouldst not," said our Lord Jesus Christ to Peter. (John xxi., 18. When such fears of death arise within us, let us gain the mastery over them, or rather let God gain it; and meanwhile, let us feel assured that we offer Him a pleasing sacrifice when we resist and do violence to our inclinations for the purpose of placing ourselves entirely under His command: This is the principle war in which

God would have His people to be engaged. He would have them strive to suppress every rebellious thought and feeling which would turn them aside from the path to which He points. And the consolations are so ample that it may well be said, we are more than cowards if we give away!

In ancient times vast numbers of people, to obtain a simple crown of leaves, refused no toil, no pain, no trouble; nay, it even cost them nothing to die, and yet every one of them fought for a peradventure, not knowing whether he was to gain or to lose the prize. God holds forth to us the immortal crown by which we may become partakers of His glory: He does not mean us to fight at haphazard, but all of us have a promise of the prize for which we strive. Have we any cause then to decline the struggle? Do we think it has been said in vain that if we die with Jesus Christ we shall also live with Him? Our triumph is prepared, and yet we do all we can to shun the combat.

But it is said that all we teach on this subject is repugnant to human judgment. I confess it. And hence when our Savior declares, "Blest are they which are persecuted for righteousness' sake" (Matt. v., 10), He gives utterance to a sentiment which is not easily received in the world. On the contrary, He wishes to account that as happiness which in the judgment of sense is misery. We seem to ourselves miserable when God leaves us to be trampled upon by the tyranny and cruelty of our enemies; but the error is that we look not to the promises of God, which assure us that all will turn to our good. We are cast down when we see the wicked stronger than we, and planting their foot on our throat; but such confusion should rather, as St. Paul says, cause us to lift up our heads. Seeing we are too much disposed to amuse ourselves with present objects, God in permitting the good to be maltreated, and the wicked to have sway, shows by evident tokens that a day is coming on which all that is now in confusion will be reduced to order. If the period seems distant, let us run to the remedy, and not flatter ourselves in our sin; for it is certain that we have no faith if we can not carry our views forward to the coming of Jesus Christ.

To leave no means which may be fitted to stimulate us unemployed, God sets before us promises on the one hand and threatenings on the other. Do we feel that the promises have not sufficient influence, let us strengthen them by adding the threatenings. It is true we must be perverse in the extreme not to put more faith in the promises of God, when the Lord Jesus says that He will own us as His before His Father, provided we confess Him before men. (Matt. x., 32; Luke xii., 8.) What should prevent us from making the confession which He requires? Let men do their utmost, they can not do worse than murder us! and will not the heavenly life compensate for this? I do not here collect all the passages in Scripture which bear on this subject: they are so often reiterated that we ought to be thoroughly satisfied with them. When the struggle comes, if three or four passages do not suffice, a hundred surely ought to make us proof against all contrary temptations.

But if God can not will us to Himself by gentle means, must we not be mere blocks if His threatenings also fail? Jesus Christ summons all those who from fear of temporal death shall have denied the truth, to appear at the bar of God his Father, and says, that then both body and soul will be consigned to perdition. (Matt. x., 28; Luke xii., 5.) And in another passage He says that He will disclaim all those who shall have denied Him before men. (Matt. x., 33; Luke xii., 10.) These words, if we are not altogether impervious to feeling, might well make our hair stand on end. Be this as it may, this much is certain; if these things do not move us as they ought, nothing remains for us but a fearful judgment. (Heb. x., 27.) All the words of Christ having proved unavailing, we stand convinced of gross infidelity.

It is in vain for us to allege that pity should be shown us, inasmuch as our nature is so frail; for it is said, on the contrary, that Moses, having looked to God by faith, was fortified so as not to yield under any temptation. Wherefore, when we are thus soft and easy to bend, it is a manifest sign, I do not say that we have no zeal, no firmness, but that we know nothing either of God or His kingdom. When we are reminded that we ought to be united to our Head, it seems to us a fine pretext for exemption to say that we are men. But what were those who have trodden the path before us? Indeed, had we nothing more than pure doctrine, all the excuses we could make would be frivolous; but having so many examples which ought to supply us with the strongest proof, the more deserving are we of condemnation.

There are two points to be considered. The first is, that the whole body of the Church in general has always been, and to the end will be, liable to be afflicted by the wicked, as is said in the Psalms (Psalms cxxix., 1), "From my youth up they have tormented me, and dragged the plow over me from one end to the other." The Holy Spirit there brings in the ancient Church, in order that we, after being much acquainted with her afflictions, may not regard it as either new or vexatious when the like is done to ourselves in the present day. St. Paul, also, in quoting from another Psalm (Rom. vii., 36; Psalm xliv., 22), a passage which says, "We have been led like sheep to the slaughter"; shows that that has not been for one age only, but is the ordinary condition of the Church, and shall be.

Therefore, on seeing how the Church of God is trampled upon in the present day by proud worldlings, how one barks and another bites, how they tortue, how they plot against her, how she is assailed incessantly by mad dogs and savage beasts, let it remind us that the same thing was done in all the olden time. It is true God sometimes gives her a truce and time of refreshment, and hence in the Psalm above quoted it is said, "He cutteth the cords of the wicked"; and in another passage (Psalm cxxv., 3), "He breaks their staff, lest the good should fall away, by being too hardly pressed." But still it has pleased Him that His Church should always have to battle so long as she is in this world, her repose being treasured up on high in the heavens. (Heb. iii., 9.)

Meanwhile, the issue of her afflictions has always been fortunate. At all events, God has caused that tho she has been prest by many calamities, she has never been completely crusht; as it is said (Psalm vii., 15), "The wicked with all their efforts have not succeeded in that at which they aimed." St. Paul glories in the fact, and shows that this is the course which God in mercy always takes. He says (I Cor. iv., 12) that we endure tribulations, but we are not in agony; we are impoverished, but not left destitute; we are persecuted, but not forsaken; cast down, but we perish not; bearing everywhere in our body the mortification of the Lord Jesus, in order that His life may be manifested in our mortal bodies. Such being, as we see, the issue which God has at all times given to the persecutions of His Church, we ought to take courage, knowing that our forefathers, who were frail men like ourselves, always had the victory over their enemies by remaining firm in endurance.

I only touch upon this article briefly to come to the second, which is more to our purpose, viz., that we ought to take advantage of the particular examples of the martyrs who have gone before us. These are not confined to two or three, but are, as the apostle says (Heb. xii., 1), "So great a cloud of witnesses." By this expression he intimates that the number is so great that it ought, as it were, completely to engross our sight. Not to be tedious, I will only mention the Jews, who were persecuted for the true religion, as well under the tyranny of King Antiochus as a little after his death. We can not allege that the number of sufferers was small, for it formed, as it were, a large army of martyrs. We can not say that it consisted of prophets whom God had set apart from common people, for women and young children formed part of the band. We can not say that they got off at a cheap rate, for they were tortured as cruelly as it was possible to be. Accordingly, we hear what the apostle says (Heb. xi., 35), that some were stretched out like drums, not caring to be delivered, that they might obtain a better resurrection; others were proved by mockery and blows, or bonds and prisons; others were stoned or sawn asunder; others traveled up and down, wandering among mountains and caves.

Let us now compare their case with ours. If they so endured for the truth which was at that time so obscure, what ought we to do in the clear light which is now shining? God speaks to us with open mouth; the great gate of the kingdom of heaven has been opened, and Jesus Christ calls us to Himself, after having come down to us that we might have him, as it were, present to our eyes. What a reproach would it be to us to have less zeal in suffering for the gospel than those who had only hailed the promises afar off—who had only a little wicket opened whereby to come to the kingdom of God, and who had only some memorial and type of Jesus Christ? These things can not be exprest in a word, as they deserve, and therefore I leave each to ponder them for himself.

The doctrine now laid down, as it is general, ought to be carried into practise by all Christians, each applying it to his own use according as may be necessary. This I say, in order that those who do not see themselves in apparent danger may not think it superfluous as regards them. They are not at this hour in the hands of tyrants, but how do they know what God means to do with them hereafter? We ought therefore to be so forearmed that if some persecution which we did not expect arrives, we may not be taken unawares. But I much fear that there are many deaf ears in regard to this subject. So far are those who are sheltered and at their ease from preparing to suffer death when need shall be that they do not even trouble themselves about serving God in their lives. It nevertheless continues true that this preparation for persecution ought to be our ordinary study, and especially in the times in which we live.

Those, again, whom God calls to suffer for the testimony of His name ought to show by deeds that they have been thoroughly trained to patient endurance. Then ought they to recall to mind all the exhortations which were given them in times past, and bestir themselves just as the soldier rushes to arms when the tempest sounds. But how different is the result. The only question is how to find out subterfuges for escaping. I say this in regard to the greater part; for persecution is a true touchstone by which God ascertains who are His. And few are so faithful as to be prepared to meet death boldly.

It is a kind of monstrous thing, that persons who make a boast of having a little of the gospel, can venture to open their lips to give utterance to such quibbling. Some will say, What do we gain by confessing our faith to obstinate people who have deliberately resolved to fight against God? Is not this to cast pearls before swine? As if Jesus Christ had not distinctly declared (Matt. viii., 38) that He wishes to be confest among the perverse and malignant. If they are not instructed thereby, they will at all events remain confounded; and hence confession is an odor of a sweet smell before God, even tho it be deadly to the reprobate. There are some who say, What will our death profit? Will it not rather prove an offense? As if God hath left them the choice of dying when they should see it good and find the occasion opportune. On the contrary, we approve our obedience by leaving in His hand the profit which is to accrue from our death.

In the first place, then, the Christian man, wherever he may be, must resolve, notwithstanding dangers or threatings, to walk in simplicity as God has commanded. Let him guard as much as he can against the ravening of the wolves, but let it not be with carnal craftiness. Above all, let him place his life in the hands of God. Has he done so?

Then if he happens to fall into the hands of the enemy, let him think that God, having so arranged, is pleased to have him for one of the witnesses of His Son, and therefore that he has no means of drawing back without breaking faith with Him to whom we have promised all duty in life and in death—Him whose we are and to whom we belong, even though we should have made no promise.

In saying this I do not lay all under the necessity of making a full and entire confession of everything which they believe, even should they be required to do so. I am aware also of the measure observed by St. Paul, altho no man was ever more determined boldly to maintain the cause of the gospel as he ought. And hence it is not without cause our Lord promises to give us, on such an occasion, "a mouth and wisdom" (Luke xxi., 15); as if he had said, that the office of the Holy Spirit is not only to strengthen us to be bold and valiant, but also to give us prudence and discretion, to guide us in the course which it will be expedient to take.

The substance of the whole is, that those who are in such distress are to ask and obtain such prudence from above, not following their own carnal wisdom, in searching out for a kind of loop-hole by which to escape. There are some who tell us that our Lord Himself gave no answer to those who interrogated Him. But I rejoin, First, That this does not abolish the rule which He has given us to make confession of our faith when so required. (I Peter iii., 15.) Secondly, That He never used any disguise to save His life: and, Thirdly, That He never gave an answer so ambiguous as not to embody a sufficient testimony to all that He had to say; and that, moreover, He had already satisfied those who came to interrogate Him anew, with the view not obtaining information, but merely of laying traps to ensnare Him.

Let it be held, then, as a fixed point among all Christians, that they ought not to hold their life more precious than the testimony to the truth, inasmuch as God wishes to be glorified thereby. Is it in vain that He gives the name of witnesses (for this is the meaning of the word martyr) to all who have to answer before the enemies of the faith? Is it not because He wished to employ them for such a purpose? Here every one is not to look for his fellow, for God does not honor all alike with the call. And as we are inclined so to look, we must be the more on our guard against it. Peter having heard from the lips of our Lord Jesus (John xxi., 18) that he should be led in his old age where he would not, asked, What was to become of his companion John? There is not one among us who would not readily have put the same question; for the thought which instantly rises in our mind is, Why do I suffer rather than others? On the contrary, Jesus Christ exhorts all of us in common, and each of us in particular, to hold ourselves "ready," in order that according as He shall call this one or that one, we may march forth in our turn.

I explained above how little prepared we shall be to suffer martyrdom, if we be not armed with the divine promises. It now remains to show somewhat more fully what the purport and aim of these promises are—not to specify them all in detail, but to show the principal things which God wishes us to hope from Him, to console us in our afflictions. Now these things, taken summarily, are three. The first is, that inasmuch as our life and death are in His hand, He will preserve us by His might that not a hair will be plucked out of our heads without His leave. Believers, therefore, ought to feel assured into whatever hands they may fall, that God is not divested of the guardianship which He exercises over their persons. Were such a persuasion well imprinted on our hearts, we should be delivered from the greater part of the doubts and perplexities which torment us and obstruct us in our duty.

We see tyrants let loose: thereupon it seems to us that God no longer possesses any means of saving us, and we are tempted to provide for our own affairs as if nothing more were to be expected from Him. On the contrary,

His providence, as He unfolds it, ought to be regarded by us as an impregnable fortress. Let us labor, then, to learn the full import of the expression, that our bodies are in the hands of Him who created them. For this reason He has sometimes delivered His people in a miraculous manner, and beyond all human expectation, as Shadrach, Meshach, and Abednego, from the fiery furnace, Daniel from the den of lions; Peter from Herod's prison, where he was locked, chained, and guarded so closely. By these examples He meant to testify that He holds our enemies in check, altho it may not seem so, and has power to withdraw us from the midst of death when He pleases. Not that He always does it; but in reserving authority to Himself to dispose of us for life and for death, He would have us to feel fully assured that He has us under His charge; so that whatever tyrants attempt, and with whatever fury they may rush against us, it belongs to Him alone to order our life.

If He permits tyrants to slay us, it is not because our life is not dear to Him, and held in a hundred times greater honor than it deserves. Such being the case, having declared by the mouth of David (Psalm cxvi., 13), that the death of the saints is precious in His sight, He says also by the mouth of Isaiah (xxvi., 21), that the earth will discover the blood which seems to be concealed. Let the enemies of the gospel, then, be as prodigal as they will of the blood of martyrs, they shall have to render a fearful account of it even to its last drop. In the present day, they indulge in proud derision while consigning believers to the flames; and after having bathed in their blood, they are intoxicated by it to such a degree as to count all the murders which they commit mere festive sport. But if we have patience to wait, God will show in the end that it is not in vain He has taxed our life at so high a value. Meanwhile, let it not offend us that it seems to confirm the gospel, which in worth surpasses heaven and earth.

To be better assured that God does not leave us as it were forsaken in the hands of tyrants, let us remember the declarations of Jesus Christ, when He says (Acts ix., 4) that He Himself is persecuted in His members. God had indeed said before, (Zech. ii., 8), "He who touches you touches the apple of mine eye." But here it is said much more expressly, that if we suffer for the gospel, it is as much as if the Son of God were suffering in person. Let us know, therefore, that Jesus Christ must forget Himself before He can cease to think of us when we are in prison, or in danger of death for His cause; and let us know that God will take to heart all the outrages which tyrants commit upon us, just as if they were committed on His own Son.

Let us now come to the second point which God declares to us in His promise for our consolation. It is, that He will so sustain us by the energy of His Spirit that our enemies, do what they may, even with Satan at their head, will gain no advantage over us. And we see how He displays His gifts in such an emergency; for the invincible constancy which appears in the martyrs abundantly and beautifully demonstrates that God works in them mightily. In persecution there are two things grievous to the flesh, the vituperation and insult of men, and the tortures which the body suffers. Now, God promises to hold out His hand to us so effectually, that we shall overcome both by patience. What He thus tells us He confirms by fact. Let us take this buckler, then, to ward off all fears by which we are assailed, and let us not confine the working of the Holy Spirit within such narrow limits as to suppose that He will not easily defeat all the cruelties of men.

Of this we have had, among other examples, one which is particularly memorable. A young man who once lived with us here, having been apprehended in the town of Tournay, was condemned to have his head cut off if he recanted, and to be burned alive if he continued steadfast to his purpose. When asked what he meant to do, he replied simply, "He who will give me grace to die patiently for His name, will surely give me grace to bear the fire." We ought to take this expression not as that of a mortal man, but as that of the Holy Spirit, to assure us that God is not less powerful to strengthen us, and render us victorious over tortures, than to make us submit willingly to a milder death. Moreover, we oftentimes see what firmness he gives to unhappy malefactors who suffer for their crimes. I speak not of the hardened, but of those who derive consolation from the grace of Jesus Christ, and by His means, with a peaceful heart, undergo the most grievous punishment which can be inflicted. One beautiful instance is seen in the thief who was converted at the death of our Lord. Will God, who thus powerfully assists poor criminals when enduring the punishment of their misdeeds, be so wanting to His own people, while fighting for His cause, as not to give them invincible courage?

The third point for consideration in the promises which God gives His martyrs is, the fruit which they ought to hope for from their sufferings, and in the end, if need be, from their death. Now, this fruit is, that after having glorified His Name—after having edified the Church by their constancy—they will be gathered together with the Lord Jesus into His immortal glory. But as we have above spoken of this at some length, it is enough here to recall it to remembrance. Let believers, then, learn to lift up their heads towards the crown of glory and immortality to which God invites them, thus they may not feel reluctant to quit the present life for such a recompense; and, to feel well assured of this inestimable blessing, let them have always before their eyes the conformity which they thus have to our Lord Jesus Christ; beholding death in the midst of life, just as He, by the reproach of the cross, attained to the glorious resurrection, wherein consists all our felicity, joy, and triumph.

END OF VOL. I.

www.ingramcontent.com/pod-product-compliance
Lightning Source LLC
Chambersburg PA
CBHW071429150426
43191CB00008B/1087